Unforgettable
Rome

A GUIDE TO 100 MASTERPIECES

© SCALA Group S.p.A., Florence
All rights reserved
Translation: Jane Waller
Maps: Igor Trovato

© Photographs: SCALA Group Photographic
Archives, Florence
Except pp. 22 (© Michael S. Yamashita/COR-
BIS), 23 (© Arte & Immagini srl/CORBIS), 74-
75 (ADP - su Licenza Fratelli Alinari), 76-77,
124 (© FOTO Vasari, Roma), 125 (Corbis),
172-179 (Foto Musei Vaticani), 216-217 (Bil-
darchiv Monheim).

Illustrations, selected from the Scala Archives,
of property belonging to the Italian Republic
are published by concession of the competent
authority (Ministero per i Beni e le Attività
Culturali).

ISBN: 183-88-8117-242-9

Printed by: Grafiche Flaminia,
Foligno (PG), 2007

Unforgettable
Rome

A GUIDE TO 100 MASTERPIECES

texts by *Giovanna Uzzani*
edited by *Claudio Strinati*

SCALA

Introduction

"Rome should be seen as one city succeeding another, and not simply in terms of the new following the antique, but also the constant succession of different epochs of new and old". Such were the words, in 1786, of the illustrious tourist Johann Wolfang Goethe. He had realised that the full appreciation of each period of figurative culture depended on the preceding one being taken into consideration, right back to remote times. Rome, which can be endlessly decoded, has a leitmotif which runs through and connects everything: the antique. Classicism in all its forms is a constant point of reference in Roman figurative culture. There are some areas of Rome where time seems to stand still and one can walk or stand in admiration in front of antique monuments or ruins which are still impressive, trying to conjure up the past. In the extraordinary continuity of life in the "eternal city", the passing of the centuries and the succession of events and peoples have transformed the urban space. Some antique constructions can be seen as they once were, although sometimes their significance has been misunderstood or changed for long periods of time, as in the case of temples transformed into Christian churches. Other buildings have been abandoned and, in the course of time, buried under accumulated layers, until being brought to light by excavations, carried out either on the evidence contained in antique sources or simply through maintenance works or whilst providing the services needed in a modern city. Whole complexes have been intentionally obliterated and covered over in the implementation of new urban plans, or dismantled, from late antiquity onwards, in order to salvage materials, especially precious marbles and metals, which have at from time to time served in the building of new architectural jewels like the baroque churches. Lastly, the expanding metropolis has engulfed monuments which were once situated on the edge or outside the urban the modern buildings or immersed in the green of the evocative archeological areas. By visiting the interior of certain single buildings, the entire architectural culture of the city from the Middle Ages to the present day can be visually reconstructed. Thus a medieval bell tower can live side by side with a baroque façade, a stately Renaissance doorway with a lavish rococò balcony, a Roman capital with a classic column. All the same, if one had to sum up the face, style and "form" of modern Rome, one word would suffice: "baroque". Carlo Maderno, Gian Lorenzo Bernini, Francesco Borromini – these are the architects who have changed, turned upside down and reinvented the city's look. With the seventeenth century urban revival, the square, which had evolved into an open and dynamic space was transformed into a stage of papal power, taking on an aspect which seems completely compatible with the ideology of triumphal catholicism. The baroque square changes the capital's urban structure: a dynamic space which the church façades, palaces and monumental buildings look onto, it becomes a theatre for the ephemeral side of the city. Crowds gather here for solemn religious occasions, theatrical and musical shows and during the investiture of the public and the powerful. The fountains have a specific role in the process of urban change in which the squares became baroque and theatrical, especially those of Gian Lorenzo Bernini. Water, movement, sound and transparency define these "creations of nature", images of vitality and energy. The Barcaccia in Piazza di Spagna, the Fontana del Tritone in Piazza Barberini, the "exhibition" piece for the Aqua Vergine aquaduct and the Fontana dei Quattro Fiumi in Piazza Navona are all emblematic examples. The baroque face of the city lives on as the centuries pass, even when it is tampered with, covered up, disowned: it lived side by side with the new inventions of neoclassical culture in the course of the XVIII century, was revived in nineteenth century bourgeois building and accompanied the solemn rationalism of the twentieth century until today it provides inspiration for experimentation in contemporary architecture. the presence of antiquity is also strongly felt in the works of art in the palaces, the churches and the museums of the capital; it is evident in the architecture as well as the succession of styles. Traces of the antique can be glimpsed in medieval fragments, just as the 15th century refined, antiquarian culture left its mark under the frescoes and funerary monuments in the churches and in the heart of pontifical power: the Vatican Palaces. The antique is part and parcel of great Renaissance art, both in the painting of Raphael and the works of Michelangelo, and was fundamental in the decorative renovation of 17th and 18th century churches and houses of the nobility, which today bear the sign, form and image par excellence of Rome. Even Caravaggio, who brought about his realism revolution, still pays homage to antiquity. Neo-classicism, the age of the Grand Tour and then the academic culture of the early 19th century, still regard Rome as the privileged cradle of artistic production. In the shadow of antiquity, and with the benefit of Renaissance texts, artists from all over Europe come here to train and leave their works behind. When the romantic revolution and the collapse of the Pontifical state begin to make Paris and London the preferred goals, Rome loses this centrality but remains a point of reference, an essential yardstick for the Pre-Raphaelites to Art Nouveau, from the monumental arch of the 20 years of fascism to the reactions of 20th century expressionism and abstract art. The only way to find and rediscover the various-sized pieces of Roman art from the Middle Ages to the 20th century is to become immersed in the colour and forms of works kept in the city's churches, which are the true palimpsests of the memory, to scour the annals of the great 17th and 18th century collections in the palaces and villas of the nobility and to tell the stories of the many works kept in the museums. This is how the threads of a unique culture can be drawn together, the unrepeatable heritage of a timeless art.

Central rioni: Palatine, Esquiline and Oppius Hills

Piazza
di Spagna

17

16

14 15

Quirinale

13

12

11

10

npidoglio

9

18

19

20

21-22

7-8

6

Colosseo

4

5

Foro Romano

3

2

1

San Giovanni in Laterano

The Lateran cathedral is part of the first monumental complex of the Church of Rome. It was built at the time of Constantine on the site of the ruined home of a powerful Roman family, the Laterani. It consists of a Papal Palace, Basilica and Baptistery, or so-called Patriarchìo, which was used for the diplomatic, residential, defence and administrative purposes of the Pontifical Curia. Until 1300, when Boniface VIII announced the first Jubilee Year, the pontiff resided here with all his dignitaries and the court, enjoying the use of a personal chapel, part of which still exists with the name of Sancta Sanctorum. The building was commissioned by Constantine as a votive offering for the victory over Maxentius, and dedicated to Christ the Saviour in 318 AD. Its blueprint was exactly the same as that of the former Saint Peter's. It must have consisted of a huge space with five aisles divided up by an impressive colonnade. After being damaged several times over the centuries, the Constantine basilica was repeatedly restored until being rebuilt by Francesco Borromini, who gave it its definitive form. In fact the monumental prospect of San Giovani in Laterano is an attempt at combining several architectural languages, with its stately pilasters shielding the five entrance doors which correspond to the five aisles of the basilica. The fifth door on the right, with the cross set in the middle of it, is the Holy Door, which is only opened every twenty-five years on the occasion of the Jubilee. In its spatial proportions the Borrominian cathedral is a faithful copy of the late antique building. In fact it was a condition of the rebuilding commissioned by Pope Innocent on the occasion of the Jubilee in 1650, that the architect Borromini should preserve the original structure of the basilica, saving the wooden ceiling, the five aisle layout and the Martin V Cosmatesque floor. So Borromini devised a large nave with side openings of five big arches separated by gigantic piers, which comprised the columns of the Constantinian complex. The Piazza San Giovanni in Laterano of today is both one of the richest parts of the city in terms of historical memories, and possibly amongst those most tampered with in the development of the modern city. A destination for pilgrims and tourists from all over the world, it contains an almost complete synthesis of Roman architectural culture in the form of its monuments, from the Egyptian obelisk to the impressive Imperial age remains, from the Paleo-Christian to the Romanesque, from the late Renaissaince to the Baroque, up to nineteenth and twentieth century historicism.

Stories of San Silvestro
Quattro Santi Coronati, Oratory of San Silvestro

The Oratory of San Silvestro, which is part of the Basilica of the Quattro Santi Coronati, was dedicated in 1246 by Cardinal Rinaldo, Bishop of Ostia. The frescoes are first and foremost an easily-read political propaganda manifesto intended to confirm the supremacy of the Pope over the emperors at a particularly difficult moment when the church was under threat from Frederick II. Once inside the little Oratory, the faithful were meant to begin with the lunette of the original entrance wall and the fresco of Christ enthroned, flanked by the Virgin, Saint John and the apostles, depicted hieratically in two groups of six. The image of Christ in Judgement therefore dominates the events narrated in the section underneath. The legend of the conversion of Constantine by Silvester I, Pope from 314 to 335, appears in the panels below. These are framed by two bands decorated with interlaced circle motifs, containing busts of the prophets

and leaves. Having met the Emperor, Silvester baptises him, immersing him in a large bath. In the following scene, the climax of the tale, kneeling before the enthroned Silvester, Constantine proffers the symbols of papal power while the royal procession looks on.

Many have commented on the fact that this cycle is stylistically still in keeping with Byzantine culture despite the changes that had already been appearing in contemporary figurative culture in Rome. Nonetheless the anonymous artist displays a lively narrative capacity, endowing the scenes with a fairy-tale-like, and, at times, expressionistic quality. The emotions of the characters are clearly visible, as in the case of the mothers who plead with the Emperor not to sacrifice their children, or the face of the sleeping Constantine, distorted by the pain of illness. Care has also been taken with the accuracy of decorative details, like the finely chiselled garments of the Emperor and the

architectural backgrounds, which, even though they appear flat, reveal the intention on the part of the fresco artist to create a realistic setting.

Donation of Constantine. *Three messengers reach the Pope.*

San Clemente

In the Basilica of San Clemente, which was built at the beginning of the XIIth century, the ancient paintings from the first early Christian basilica have survived and most of the apse and arch mosaics are intact. The main subject of the cycle of frescoes dating back to the end of the XIth century, in the present lower church, is the celebration of the titular saint: the martyr Pope of the primitive church, Clemente. The episodes relating to the life of the saint are portrayed in the nave. The cycle also includes stories from the other saints, including the legend of Saint Alessio. These frescoes were rediscovered during excavations carried out in the new medieval church, at the end of the XIXth century, and constitute important evidence

of figurative Roman culture between the XIth and XIIth centuries, as well as providing information on the original appearance of the early Christian basilica. The cycle introduces new features in Roman painting at the turn of the XIth century: narrative immediacy, the expressive distortion caused by the emphasis of emotions, and the appearance of naturalistic colouring. On the whole, the frescoes constitute a more sophisticated version of catacomb painting, both in their use of the expressive and dynamic line and in their revival, in the early Christian sense, of decorative motifs, which are inserted in preordained architectural frameworks. In the bowl-shaped apse there are extraordinarily well-

Top: interior; left: apse.

preserved mosaics representing the Cross as Tree of Life, at the top of the hill of Paradise. There are depictions of the doves, symbols of the soul, and, at the base of the Cross, there are two elegant deer drinking from the river and a phoenix, symbols of immortality. The central scene of the Crucifixion combines a more modern, direct and explicit vision with a stately, abstract symbolism. Above the tree, the hand of God the Father is depicted in a star-studded sphere, which is symbolic of the glory of the Lord. In the basilica, in the chapel of Saint Catherine, there is also a fine cycle of Renaissance frescoes by the painter Masolino da Panicale, portraying Stories from Saint Catherine and Saint Ambrose. The pictorial language is based on a knowledge of Brunelleschian perspective but the painting is refined and elegant, thanks to the delicately toned light and a tendency towards a welcome naturalism, as in the tender modelling of the bodies.

Masolino, *The Martyrdom of the Saint, Stories of Saint Catherine,* Cappella di Santa Caterina.

Colosseum

From the moment it was built, the grandeur of the Flavian Amphitheatre has conditioned Rome's urban landscape and it still dominates the ancient centre. Its arcaded surface was chosen as the theatrical background to the Via dei Fori Imperiali. It was the first amphitheatre to be built in Rome in the form of a monument. In the Republican age the gladiatorial games took place in the Roman Forum, where temporary wooden structures were provided for the occasion.

Vespasian, the founder of the Flavian dynasty, emerged victorious from the civil war which followed Nero's death in 69AD. As part of a coherent political scheme, the new Emperor decided to dedicate the huge urban spaces and works of art appropriated by Nero to the public, for their enjoyment. The inhabitants of Rome must have appreciated the building of the big amphitheatre in the centre of the valley, which had previously been the site of the artificial lake made for Nero. The Judaic

war, which had ended in 70 AD with the destruction of the temple of Jerusalem, provided the booty and the manpower needed for the construction of the building. It was Vespasian's son, Titus, who inaugurated the amphitheatre in 80 AD, with a memorable gala and games lasting 100 days. The Flavian Amphitheatre was superior in dimensions and monumentality to all those previously built. It was 52 m high, like the northern side near the Via dei Fori Imperiali, which is still intact. The

whole of the external wall was faced with marble slabs and decorated with statues in the arcades, and bronze shields hung from the attic storey windows. The organisation of the internal seating was strictly governed by the laws established by Augustus, through which spectators were seated according to their social class. The Colosseum was furnished with a sophisticated system of drains which fed the baths and numerous fountains required to keep the vast audience cool. In the amphitheatre there were various kinds of entertainment: fights between pairs of gladiators, hunts involving wild and exotic animals, naval battles and capital punishment executions by exposure to wild beasts, which were also suffered by Christians during periods of persecution. The losers could ask the master of ceremonies, whose decision often depended on the mood of the audience, for mercy. Once the building fell into disuse it gradually deteriorated, and in the Middle Ages dwellings and a fortress were built

inside it. The marble facing was systematically removed. Since its redisovery in the Renaissance, the Colosseum has been one of the monuments which symbolise the grandeur of antique Rome.

Arch of Constantine

The arch, as a type of monument, was well suited to celebrating the ventures and victories, firstly of the consuls in the Republican age and, later on, of the emperors. It was much used in Rome, which is studded with numerous monuments of this type. The arches, which underwent an architectural and stylistic evolution in the course of the centuries, generally either spanned a street or were placed near the entrance of a monumental zone. The bloody civil battle fought on the Milvian Bridge at the gates of Rome on October 28th 312 AD, would determine whether Constantine or Maxentius was to have absolute control of the empire. After the victory, and the death of the rival on the battlefield, on the ancient triumphal road in the valley of the Colosseum between the Flavian amphitheatre and the Roman Forum, an honorary arch was erected in honour of Constantine. It is the largest to have survived in Rome, has three arches and is adorned with reliefs and sculptures. The huge monument was the symbolic counterpart of the mere rite of ceremonial entry of the Emperor into Rome. In fact, on the eve of the decisive battle, Constantine had had the famous vision of the cross with the inscription «with this sign you will win», an event which prompted him to place the monogram of Christ on the soldiers' shields and which marked the moment he turned towards Christianity. The Arch of Constantine is all of 21m high and is built of white marble and articulated in three openings, the middle being the largest. It is flanked by protruding Corinthian columns in antique yellow. Reuse of sculptures or structures from the preceding age was commonplace, and celebratory sculptures were inserted in the arch to enrich the figurative decoration. At the sides of the inscription on the attic storey, there are four rectangular reliefs on each façade, originating from an arch of the Emperor Marcus Aurelius. The eight statues of Dacian prisoners placed in the attic storey against the columns date back to the Trajan age, as do the four stone slabs extracted from a big battle-scene frieze, on the sides of the storey and inside the central arch. Here they are crowned with the inscriptions «to the founder of peace» and «to the liberator of the city», referring to Contantine's victory over Maxentius.

Domus Aurea

In 64BC, a devastating fire, for which the Emperor Nero was not entirely blameless, destroyed most of Rome. The reconstruction of the city encompassed the building of his own residence in the grand style. A huge part of the centre of Rome was transformed into a vast residential area, almost like a city within a city. «A single house took over the "Urbs" (City)», claims Martial, and Suetonius refers to scornful verses which were displayed around the stunned city: «Rome is turning into a house! Migrate to Veio or Quiriti, provided the house doesn't extend as far as Veio». The residence was planned to occupy an area of between 60 and 80 hectares and extend from the Palatine to the Velia, where the vestibule with the bronze Colossus was, and from the Oppius hill to the valley of the Colosseum and as far as the Coelian hills. The Domus Aurea was not formed of a single palace, but of separate pavillions linked by porticos and terraces and scattered over a wide area, along the same architectural lines as the villa, which was at that time only found outside Rome. It included cultivated fields, vineyards, meadows, pasture, and woods full of wild as well as tame animals. The building revolved around a series of terraces which rose from the valley with its artificial lake (the future site of the Colosseum) up the slopes of the Oppius. The main body of the complex consisted of five areas radiating from the pivot of the famous Octagonal Hall. These, together with the central nymphaenum, were illuminated by the light which passed firstly through the huge central eye and then through windows cut in the walls below. The marble-clad walls

both reflected light and created a sense of lightness. The Octagon may have been the round banqueting hall described in sources, with an ingenious mechanism which revolved day and night, displaying various images. Liberal use of gold-leaf in the frescoes and stucco-work which decorated the interiors was part and parcel of Nero's ideological programme. At the heart of this were worship of the Sun God, with whom the Emperor himself identified, and the launching of a new golden age, from which the name of the residence originated.

View of the Nymphaenum   View of the
of Poliremus.   Octagonal Hall.

San Pietro in Vincoli

Legend has it that when Eudoxia, wife of the Emperor Valentinian III, received the chains which had bound the apostle Peter in Jerusalem, she gave them to Saint Leo the Great, who put them beside the chains which had bound the apostle in Rome. Miraculously the two chains fused together and this chain is still kept in the Basilica of San Pietro in Vincoli. Athough the early-Christian origins of the complex can be identified in the crypt, the building of today is Renaissance in appearance, starting from the fifteenth century portico made from 20 ancient marble Doric columns. The fifteenth and sixteenth century paintings of Antoniazzo Romano, Domenichino and Guercino are still kept inside the basilica. In the right-hand transept is the towering mausoleum of Pope Julius II Della Rovere, by Michelangelo, which has since been granted the architectural frame the artist had always intended for it. The placing of a big lunette behind the monument causes powerful natural light to illuminate the sculpture from behind, endowing it with a mystic aura and enhancing the chiaroscuro. During the eighteenth century, this source of light had been obscured by opalescent glass which made the marble monument seem flat and no different from other funerary monument prototypes. After recent restoration, a medieval fresco was also discovered at the vestry entrance, behind the monument to Julius II, and its proper display was provided for when Michelangelo's original plans were implemented.

Michelangelo, Moses
San Pietro in Vincoli

The coveted commission of his own splendid mausoleum by Julius II turned into an utter tragedy for Michelangelo, thanks to the continuous interruptions and endless modifications to which the original design was subject. Michelangelo threw himself into the project with great enthusiasm, following the first plan. This envisaged a mausoleum of three storeys decorated with forty statues in marble, and bronze reliefs; the Moses was to form a pendant to the statue of Saint Paul, both being symbols of the mystery of God's revelation. Having spent a considerable time on producing numerous drawings and studies, as well as choosing the marbles in Carrara, the sculptor was forced to abandon the project and concentrate firstly on the work in Saint Peter's, to which Julius II apparently gave precedence, and, after that, on the ceiling of the Sistine Chapel. When the Pope died in 1513, Michelangelo returned to the project, although it had been very much reduced and modified; the mausoleum was no longer free-standing but attached to the walls and it had fewer statues. The artist undertook to finish this second project within seven years, but, in fact, thirty years would pass before the end product of the tomb in San Pietro in Vincoli was achieved, work on this having only been resumed in 1532 after a long interruption. Between 1513 and 1515 Michelangelo worked on the statues of the first two Prisoners (today in the Louvre), which should have acted as telamons to hold up the architrave beside the two figures of Victories, and that of Moses. The latter undoubtedly represents one of the summits of Michelangelo's art in terms of expressiveness. The rough, nervy quality of the marble surfaces reflects the interior strength, as well as the apprehension, of the prophet of Hebrew Law, symbol of the human condition. Hints of antique culture – from the Torso of the Belvedere to the figures of ancient river divinities – blend with echoes from fifteenth century sculpture, particularly that of Donatello. The figure is seated, the face contracted in concentration and turned towards the left; the right foot rests on the ground, while the left leg is raised with only the point of the foot resting on the base. The biblical figure has a majestic, solemn air in spite of the pervasive feeling of dynamism and withheld energy.

9

Maxentius Basilica

The monument, built at the behest of Maxentius in 308 AD, was formerly known as the Basilica Nova or Basilica Costantiniana in reference to the Emperor Constantine, who finished building it. The building was probably the seat of the judicial activity of the praefectus urbi, who controlled the entire judicial and administrative activity of the city from the beginning of the Vth century. In the same period, the seat of the tribunal, where cases concerning senators were heard behind closed doors, was transferred here. Over the centuries the basilica was stripped of its precious elements of architectural furnishing and it is likely that, during the VIIth century, Pope Honorius removed the gilded bronze tiles to use them to cover the roof of Saint Peter's. The ruin of the monument was mainly caused by several earthquakes. The basilica covered most of Velia and a vast portion of the monumental area in the Roman Forum. The choice of the place, which is highly significant in terms of ancient Roman history, was a reflection of deep political and ideological values. Maxentius, carrying on from where his father Maximian Hercules left off, initiated an intense programme of building activity. In terms of the creation of monuments in the grand style, the basilica had an important role in the scheme. The preparation of its site entailed the demolition of the impressive spice store-houses built by Domitian and the removal of another part of the hill of Velia (which had already been modified by Nero for the construction of the Domus Aurea). After the death of Maxentius, who was defeated in 312 AD near the Milvio Bridge, the basilica was perfected by the Emperor Constantine. It has a rectangular plan (100 x 65 m) and was articulated by an ample 35 metre high nave, roofed by three groin vaults resting on eight marble

columns, with a large apse at the end. In 1613, Pope Paul Vth placed the only surviving column in the middle of Piazza Sant Maria Maggiore, where it can still be seen today, forming a base for the statue of the Madonna. Besides the architectural design, the interior furnishings of the basilica were conceived as an expression of the grandiosity of the monument and, at the same time, emphasised the power and magnificence of the Emperor.

Imperial Forums

The Imperial Forums were built after Caesar's Forum in Hellenistic style and were conceived as a single architectural project rather than being the result of a series of irregular juxtapositions as in the case of the Roman Forum. The complex owes its monumentality and unique character to its decorative array and the perimeter wall which kept vehicles out. Extensive excavations took place in the Imperial Forums in the 1930s, when the Via dell'Impero, now Via dei Fori Imperiali,

was constructed. It was opened in October 1932 as a means of exalting and legitimising the noble Roman origins of the Fascist stock. Other town planning projects were intended to make similar statements, like the monumental opening of the Via della Conciliazione. Today the road still cuts the archeological area in half, concealing important structures, such as the entrance to the Forum of Augustus. Excavations, which were resumed in 1995, were carried out along scientific lines.

The recovery of thousands of square metres of buried sites has made it possible to attain a more perfect reconstruction of the appearance of the monumental centre in the Imperial Age and also to document the subsequent history of the area, which was used for housing in the early Middle Ages.

Mercati Traianei

The huge architectural complex of the forum and Trajan's Markets was until late antiquity considered the most famous of Rome's wonders. The impressive project was attributed to Apollodorus of Damascus, a Syrian architect, who worked mainly under the Emperor Trajan, in the first half of the second century AD.

This architect, one of the few artists of whom records survive, fused and reworked the fundamental principles of Hellenistic and Roman architecture. The Markets, which were designed at the same time as Trajan's forum, are set on the slopes of the Quirinale, with a series of superimposed terraces. The removal of part of the hill, to a height equivalent to that of Trajan's column, had made space for the creation of a piazza (square) in the grand style. The complex, which was designed for commercial and storage use, is articulated on different levels, and its façade consists of a large exedra (curving wall), which includes the Forum's eastern side, with eleven tabernae (booths) facing it.

The third level consists of a terrace, with more stalls placed along a well-preserved ancient road: the Via Biberatica. This road led to a monumental hall which was the focal point of the complex: it was two storeys high, with a cross-vaulted roof in the grand style and two floors of tabernae. The south side of the hall leads into a series of rooms which were probably dedicated to the administrative offices.

The name Via Biberatica probably originates from the Latin noun biber (drink) and may be connected to the trade particular to the booths, possibly taverns, which lined it. The well-preserved road

runs straight until it is cut off by the embankment of the modern quarter of Via Quattro Novembre, then follows the curve of the exedra in the direction of the Subura, the most famous and infamous popular quarter of Rome, which occupied the valley between the Quirinale and the Esquiline Hill.

There were about a hundred of the small tabernae, partly leaning straight against the rock of the hill. Trajan's Markets were the focal point of the city's commercial activity, with trading taking place within the booths, exactly as in modern commercial centres.

Caesar's Forum

At the end of the first century BC there were so many sacred and civic buildings as well as honorary monuments in the ancient Roman Forum that the area could no longer accommodate the amount of economic, political and judiciary activities carried on in its midst. Julius Caesar was the first to realise the need to expand the city's monument by having another piazza built at his own expense. It was named after him: the Forum Iulium or Caesar's Forum, as it was called in the sources. The urban project was of fundamental importance to the future history of this area of Rome. In fact it was Caesar (54-46 BC) who chose its significant position near the Republican forum and thus determined the layout of the other four piazzas which were built by successive emperors: the Forum of Augustus (42-2 AD), the Temple of Peace conceived by Vespasiano (71-75 AD), the Forum of Nerva (80-97 AD) and Trajan's Forum (106-112 AD). These, together with Caesar's Forum, make up the archeological area in the heart of the city, which is nowadays known as the Imperial Forums. In 54 BC, while he was engaged in military campaigns, Caesar entrusted Cicero and other intermediaries with the task of buying houses and land in the quarter behind the Roman Forum, to build his piazza. A huge sum was spent, between 60 and 100 million sestertius, according to ancient authors. The complex was inaugurated in 46 BC, to celebrate the triple victory of the leader over Gaul, Egypt and Africa, although Augustus finished it. The whole of the piazza, which is rectangular in form (160 by 75 m), was uncovered during excavations. It was paved with travertine stone and surrounded on three sides by porticos, dominating the piazza as a focal point in terms of perspective.

Colonna Traiana

The column decorated with historical scenes is a form of monument particular to Rome, and was introduced for the first time in Trajan's forum by the architect Apollodorus of Damascus, who was in charge of the whole project. The reliefs carved on the column are presented in sequence, winding round the shaft up to the top, as a narrative tale, in celebration of the feats and triumphs of the Emperor. The column was dedicated to Trajan in 113AD by the Senate and the people of Rome, in the forum bearing the same name. The height of the monument (about 40m) matches the one on the hill, which was dismantled when the complex of the Markets and the Forum was built, as the inscription on the base of the column states. The top of the monument was crowned with a bronze statue of Trajan which has not survived; it was replaced by one of Saint Peter in 1588. The base is in the form of an altar similar to the funerary altars of the Republican Age, and it served as a tomb for the Emperor; Trajan's ashes were kept in a gold urn placed in the burial chamber inside the base of the column. Here there is a hall leading to a spiral staircase made of marble, with 185 steps leading from the base to the top of the monument. Termed a cochlite column, like that of Marcus Aurelius, due to the presence of a spiral within the shaft, it was conceived by Trajan's architect, Apollodorus of Damascus. On the outside, the long spiral frieze recounts the two Dacian campaigns with a figure of Victory writing on a shield separating them, but no attempt to create a link between them. The crossing of the Danube by the Roman army on a bridge of boats marks the

beginning of the wars, and there follow battles, sieges, the setting up of encampments, the placing of troops and the submission of the indigenous chiefs to the Emperor.

Facing page:
Detail from Trajan's Column: The Emperor making a sacrifice in front of the bridge over the Danube.

14

Melozzo da Forlì,
frescoes in the Palazzo del Quirinale

«He was very learned in matters of art, and was very methodical and diligent when it came to foreshortening, as can be seen in Sant'Apostolo in Rome, in the apse containing the main altar[…] where the foreshortening of the figure of Christ is executed so well that it seems to pierce the ceiling, as do the angels, who in varying attitudes fly through the air». This passage from the Lives of Giorgio Vasari is one of the first pieces of evidence referring to the frescoes painted by Melozzo da Forli for the apse of the Chiesa dei Santi Apostoli. Unfortunately they were destroyed during renovation carried out by the architect Francesco Fontana at the time of Pope Clement XI, between 1702 and 1711. Today, some fragments kept in the Pinacoteca Vaticana and the Quirinale are all that is left of this important cycle; it was the first prestigious Roman commission undertaken by Melozzo in Rome, where he probably arrived in 1470. As Vasari mentioned, it is the foreshortening, from the bottom to the top, of the figure in benediction in the Christ in Glory surrounded by cherubs, which adds to its splendid monumentality. It reveals the painter's uncommon technical expertise, both in the use of a palette made up of vibrant colours which call to mind the «luminous» painting of Piero della Francesca and Beato Angelico, and in the studied perspective and clear-cut volumetric construction of the figures. From the surviving fragments one can also imagine how these figures, the festive choir of angels and the semicircle of Apostles looking up towards Jesus, stood out against the vivid lapislazuli blue background, unconfined by architectural frames.

15

Sant'Andrea al Quirinale

With its gilding, marbles, stucco-work and original elliptical layout, Sant'Andrea al Quirinale is one of the masterpieces of sacred Baroque architecture.

On the site of the previous sixteenth century church, Sant'Andrea a Montecavallo, building started on the new temple for the novitiate of the Jesuits in 1658, at the behest of Alessandro VII Chigi. Camillo Pamphili was the patron and Gian Lorenzo Bernini the architect. Construction advanced rapidly and it was completely finished in 1678. It is one of the richest and most harmonious examples of the Baroque architecture of Gian Lorenzo Bernini, and in a very different style from the similar «Borrominian» Baroque masterpiece, San Carlino alle Quattro Fontane. Certain elements are taken from sixteenth century architecture, but they are given a new slant by Bernini, as in the case of the monumental single tier façade,

with its Corinthian pilasters supporting a triangular pediment, which has a large semicircular window in the middle.

The whole gives the impression that the porch resting on ionic columns is upside down. The superb interior, based on that of the Pantheon, has an elliptical plan, with the main axis perpendicular to that of the entrance.

The radial chapels are set back so as not to interrupt the unbroken oval shape, and the impression of spatial airiness is accentuated by the overall diffused luminosity which emanates from the numerous windows in the dome and the lantern.

The light brings out the decorative richness of the interior, with its alternating polychrome marbles, gilding and stucco-work, designed by Bernini himself and executed by Antonio Raggi and others between 1661 and 1666.

Above, Antonio Raggi,
Sant'Andrea in Gloria.
Left, façade of the church.

Following pages, vault of the cupola.

San Carlo alle Quattro Fontane

For Francesco Borromini, the young architect from Tocino who arrived in Rome in about 1620, the project of the church and convent of San Carlino alle Quattro Fontane, which was commissioned by the Order of the Trinitarians, was decisive, coming as it did after the success of his involvement in Palazzo Barberini. In1634 Borromini set in motion the building of the convent, which was finished two years later; the church, on the other hand, took longer to complete, as it was begun in 1638 and only finished in 1667. The prospect is animated by an ingenious play of volumes and lines determined by the contrast of concave and convex surfaces. Then there is the elliptical dome with concave niches in the lantern, and, on the left side, the bell tower with its convex belfry and pointed roof. The alternating use of ellipsis and oval, concave and convex elements endows the façade with vigour and gives the impression that it is in continuous rotation. The internal space is limited; nonetheless this minuscule, compressed space is the most powerful expression of Borromini's sculptural architecture. The space, which seems minimal at first, teems with the richest and most refined decorations taken from nature: capitals covered in leaves, altar cornices fashioned in the form of bunches of flowers, luxuriant and fleshy friezes of acanthus, culminating in the oval dome. Here the ingeniousness of Borromini makes the structures appear moulded and almost carved, with its unprecedented attention to detail. The refinement and inventiveness is enhanced by the illumination, which is not simply obtained by light filtering from the lantern, but also from little windows placed behind the delicate stucco frieze above the impost of the dome. A tour de force of harmony and proportion, the rooms of the convent are arranged around a cloister where the innovative element of the rounded and slightly convex corners takes the rigidity out of the structures, making them relate to one another in a more articulated and lively way as parts of a whole. The way in which Borromini exploits the linear play in the cornices and the rhythm of the architectural elements in the interests of light is absolutely novel. Simplicity and magic are united in this space, which seems concentrated within a limited circumference. The innovative and ingenious style inaugurated by the works of Borromini had wide-reaching effects throughout Europe and would also have a decisive influence on modern architecture.

17

Pietro da Cortona, The Triumph of Divine Providence
Palazzo Barberini

The fresco painted by Pietro da Cortona for the ceiling in the main hall of Palazzo Barberini was the most grandiose and spectacular decorative enterprise of the time. The objective was to represent pictorially the triumph of noble lineage in which religious and worldly power are united. The Tuscan painter, who was by then highly prized in Rome, began the project between the end of 1632 and the beginning of 1633. The work, which took a long time to complete and was problematic, not least because of the interruptions owed to the artist's absences, was only finished at the end of 1639. Surrounded by heavenly allegories and mythological episodes, the centre of the composition represents the apotheosis of Providence combined with that of the Pontiff Urban VIII Barberini and his family. The vast surface of the painting, about six hundred square metres, is divided into five different areas corresponding to the five parts of heaven, by a pretence architectural frame, beyond which the open sky is resplendent. The Pontiff Barberini is fêted by the presence of the family emblem of bees crowned with laurel, which form the focal point of the composition. The pretence architectural frame inserted by Cortona is based on the idea of Annibale Carracci for the Gallery of Palazzo Farnese, but in this case the width is considerably reduced. This has the effect of heightening the illusory dimension of the background sky, turning it into a unifying element, whose luminosity pervades and integrates the five discrete sections contained in the framework. The impression is of a spectacular apparition, which assails the observer with the swirling and ceaseless grouping and dispersal of the figures, who are projected as if by magic on to the heavenly space.

18

Gian Lorenzo Bernini, Ecstasy of Saint Teresa
Santa Maria della Vittoria

In the Cappella Cornaro, Bernini accomplishes one of his most extraordinary artistic feats, creating a monument which has a remarkable theatrical and illusionistic power. The theme of the chapel was the ecstasy of the Spanish saint, Teresa, who was famed for the unusual spiritual experiences through which she attained mystic union with Christ. The artist has had no trouble portraying the saint in a state of rapture, but the pose is so sensual that the spiritual nature of the event is lost on many observers. It is as if the saint is suspended

on a bed of clouds, whose base, because it is darker and placed further back, is at first glance invisible, giving the impression that the marble cloud really is suspended in the air. However the main theatrical and illusory effect is achieved by the role Bernini so wisely gives to the natural light. Behind the sculpture, he creates a small semi-circular apse, which projects from the wall of the church. This enables him to open a window, which is invisible to people looking at the chapel, at the top of the little apse. To emphasise the symbolic value of the light, he adds a series of gilded rays, which reflect and enhance the light entering through the little window. The effect was intended to appear supernatural. Bernini had turned the chapel into a theatrical stage with many spectators: the patron, the Venetian cardinal, Federico Corsaro, and his ancestors. In their half-length portraits, they peer from the side boxes as if invited to share in the miraculous event, and seem to cast intent and admiring glances on the drama unfolding on the stage - the central group of the saint with the angel who is about to transfix her with a dart. In a sense this work is a symbol of the baroque itself: sculpture, light, architecture and painting are fused in a unique tableau of awe and wonder; tangible reality and the illusion of space are indistinguishable and art and imagination are as one.

Museo Nazionale Romano

The Museum was established in 1889 to house the antiquities of Rome and, not surprisingly, it represents the richest archeological collection in the world. The treasures are displayed in several buildings, including the Palazzo Massimo alle Terme, most of whose grounds were expropriated by the Italian State for the site of the Termini Railway Station. The building was acquired by the State in 1981 and specially adapted to accommodate the museum exhibits. The ground and first floors house a rich collection of sculptures from the Roman era, displayed in chronological order from the Republican Age to the Imperial era, such as the ivory head, the Girl of Anzio, the Crouching Aphrodite from Villa Adriana, the statue of Augustus as Pontifex Maximus, the Lancellotti Discus Thrower, and numerous portraits and reliefs. On the second floor precious examples of decorative furnishings are kept, such as the painted garden from the Villa di Livia, frescoes from the Villa Farnesina and the Rome of the Barberini, stucco-work, floor mosaics and the luxurious panels in polychrome marble from the Basilica di Giunio Basso and the Mithraeum of Santa Prisca.

Aphrodite by Doidalsas.

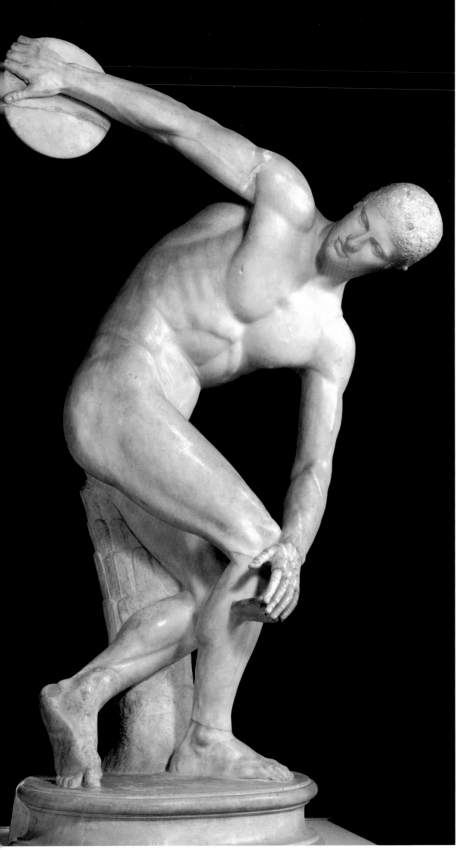

The tour of the museum is rounded off on the ground floor by the important section dedicated to coins and jewels; two items which stand out are the famous gem with the bust of Athena and the furnishings for the tomb of Grottarossa, where the mummified body of an eight-year old child was found. The Baths of Diocletian, the largest thermal complex built in Rome, were also chosen to accommodate a museum when the Museo Nazionale Romano was founded. The archeological material is displayed both in the gardens and the Michelangelo cloister of Santa Maria degli Angeli, as well as in rooms inside. The epigraphical section, which enables the history of Latin script to be traced from its first appearance, is one of the most important in existence. Worth noting among the most significant items are the large clay busts of the goddess Ceres and her daughter from Ariccia, and interesting figurative evidence of cults followed in Rome. The first floor of the cloister contains a protohistorical section, illustrating the most ancient phases of life of the Latin peoples, before the rise of Rome, with significant finds originating from recent excavations.

Discus Thrower by Myron.

20

Mosaics in Santa Prassede

The revival of the mosaic after its decline in the period of iconaclism is exemplified in the church of Santa Prassede, a Carolingian place of worship. The ornamental mosaic decoration covering the triumphal arch, the transept walls and the bowl-shaped ceiling of the apse is reminiscent of the original early-Christian mosaics in terms of ornamentation and technique. In fact the mosaics, including thematic ones, are made in the traditional Roman way, with exclusive use of glass tesserae. They are comparable to the mosaic decoration of the arch and the bowl-shaped ceiling of the apse in the chiesa di Santi Cosma e Damiano. The number and positioning of the characters portrayed, the choice of colours and the relation between the mosaics and their architectural context, all call to mind the basilica which sprang up in the Forum. The iconographic scheme of the apse ceiling has Christ in the middle, surrounded by saints and Pope Paschal I, who is carrying the model of the building. In the section beneath, the background of the procession of lambs, which converges on the lamb of Christ, is gold. For the lamb of God, on the other hand, in an almost unprecedented example in the Rome of the early Middle Ages - silver being very rare at the time - silver tesserae are used for the halo. At the end of the nave, in the triumphal arch, Jerusalem is conjured up in rich and splendid materials. Inside the walls of the city, which is symbolic of eternal salvation, Christ is portrayed between two angels, the Apostles and Saints. At the gates of the city, angels receive the Blessed, who tread on flower-covered ground. In the background is a splendid, bright blue,

cloud-filled sky. The decoration of the Cappella di San Zenone, one of the finest votive chapels the early Middle Ages has left us, is derived from late antique figurative schemes. Inside, a sea of gold emanates from the background of all the mosaics except at the top of the ceiling, where Christ, in golden garments, stands out against the dense blue of the background. The barrel-vaulting is adorned with plant volute decoration containing

many animals, including deer, storks and lions, a widely-used motif taken from classical art.

Madonna with Child between Saints Prassede and Pudenziana. Cappella di San Zenone.

Santa Prassede, detail of the face.

Saint Mary Major

The basilica built on the northern summit of the Esquiline Hill was originally known as Santa Maria; it was the first basilica in Rome to be named after the Virgin. In the course of the centuries, with the proliferation of the number of places of worship dedicated to the Madonna in Rome, the name never changed, but the adjective Maior was added in the Carolingian age. According to legend, Pope Liberius traced the outline of the complex after a miraculous snowfall as long ago as 358AD. However, it was in the Vth century, with Sixtus III, that the basilica attained the status of the first great building of the Church of Rome, thanks to its guiding role, as well as its central position on the site of the ancient forum and at the point of convergence of main routes. Its status is justified, given the grand style and opulence of the internal decoration, which was given a didactic role. The façade was devised by Ferdinando Fuga in about 1743 and articulated in such a way as to incorporate the mosaics of the first façade. Behind the façade is the soaring bell tower; it is the highest in Rome and, in terms of articulation, it is the last and most monumental in the mould of the Latian Romanesque prototype. Five monumental entrances embellished with pillars bearing Corinthian capitals lead to the front portico. Inside, the nave, whose walls are decorated with the important Vth century mosaic cycle, ends in a monumental Sistine triumphal arch and a XIIIth century apse. A classical frieze extends right round the basilica under the wooden ceiling. The iconographic and decorative scheme implemented in the late sixteenth century

by Sixtus V was expressly devoted to the glorification of the figure of the Virgin, whose maternity the Council of Trent had attributed to divinity, contrary to the affirmations of the Protestant Reformation. The walls of the Sistine chapel, like the Pauline chapel in the left aisle, which was designed to house the revered sacred icon of the Madonna, are decorated with a profusion of marbles salvaged from buildings of the Roman era and the former Palazzo Apostolico.

22

Mosaics of Saint Mary Major

The Rome of the Middle Ages was the main centre of production in terms of the ancient tradition of mosaic decoration. In buildings of Christian worship it is the walls and ceilings with their thousands of tesserae of coloured stones which are most resplendent, rather than the floors with their customary repertoire of geometric designs. They are mainly Hellenistic in taste, but later the designs become less plastic and more manifestly «impressionistic». The Vth century mosaics of the triumphal arch and nave in Saint Mary Major are particularly fine, with their distinctive, stately manner ushering in the first phase of the Byzantine style. Here the history of the Hebrew people is intended to represent the history of all humanity before the advent of the Redeemer. Many of the mosaicists who were active in Saint Mary Major probably drew their inspiration for the cycle from illuminated manuscripts, to judge from their classical style, the pattern and sequencing of the scenes, and the economy in the definition of the landscapes which form the backgrounds of the compositions. The mosaic in the apse of Saint Mary Major was later renewed in the time of Pope Nicholas IV (1288-1292). Active in Rome between 1291 and 1300, the painter Jacopo Torriti probably trained in the Papal City in the circle of Cimabue. Having executed the apse mosaic in San Giovanni in Laterano, in 1295 he was working on the large mosaic with the Coronation and Stories of the Virgin for Saint Mary Major. Noone knows to what extent Torriti drew inspiration from the previous apse decoration for the iconographic composition, but there is a Byzantine archaism about the work, especially in the iconographic and ornamental references to more ancient Roman mosaics. The refined use of colour is in keeping with the grand style; the ornamental motifs are taken from early-Christian classicism and, in their solidity, the figures offer a unique pictorial parallel, of a more miniature, elegant and precious form, to the Roman sculptures of Arnolfo di Cambio.

Crossing the Red Sea and detail. Nave, Stories from the Old Testament.

Abraham and the Angels. Nave, Stories from the Old Testament.

Central rioni: Trevi, Colonna and Campo Marzio

23. **Piazza del Campidoglio**

24. **Santa Maria in Aracoeli**
Virgin in Benediction

25-27. **Musei Capitolini**
Spinario
Marcus Aurelius

28. **Piazza Venezia**

29-30 **The Gesù**
Baciccia, *Adoration of the Name of Jesus*

31. **Sant'Andrea della Valle**
Giovanni Lanfranco, *Frescoes*

32. **Museo Barracco**

33. **Galleria Doria Pamphilj**
Annibale Carracci, *Landscape with the Flight into Egypt*

34. **Santa Maria sopra Minerva**
Filippino Lippi, frescoes in the Cappella Carafa

35. **Pantheon**

36. **Sant'Ignazio**
Andrea Pozzo, *Glory of Saint Ignatius*

37. **Piazza Navona**

38. **San Luigi dei Francesi**
Caravaggio, *Stories of Saint Matthew*

39-41. **Palazzo Altemps**
Ludovisi Throne
The Galatian and his wife committing suicide

42. **Sant'Agostino**
Caravaggio, *Madonna dei Pellegrini*

43. **Fontana di Trevi**

44. **Palazzo Barberini**

45. **Trinità dei Monti and Piazza di Spagna**

46. **Ara Pacis**

47. **Piazza del Popolo and Santa Maria del Popolo**

48. **Santa Maria del Popolo**
Caravaggio, *Conversion of Saint Paul* and *Crucifixion of Saint Peter*

Villa Borghese

Piazza
di Spagna

Quirinale

Piazza Navona

Piazza
del Campidoglio

Colosseo

48
47
46
45
44
43
42
41
39
38
37
36
35
34
33
32
31
29-30
28
25-27
23
24

Piazza del Campidoglio

The Piazza del Campidoglio, with the long flight of steps leading up to it, is both the political and physical heart of the city. It was designed in its monumental setting by Michelangelo in 1536, under the patronage of Paul III Farnese. It arguably represents the most perfect translation of the concept of the piazza as an autonomous urban space in sixteenth century culture. In a masterly reinterpretation of the classic concept of the piazza, Michelangelo reversed the outlook, which had until then been oriented towards the Roman Forum, placing the statue of Marcus Aurelius in the middle to face Saint Peter's Basilica. As background, he devised the complete rebuilding of the medieval Palazzo Senatorio, which rose above the ruins of the former Tabularium, and the side wings, made up of the Palazzo dei Conservatori and the Palazzo Nuovo. The latter were completed according to the artist's plans respectively in 1568 and 1655. Uprooted and set obliquely, they endow the piazza with a greater sense of space, and enhance the perspective and theatricality. The geometric star design of the paving, which was implemented in 1940 by Antonio Muñoz based on the plans left by Buonarroti, also emphasises the centrifugal, dynamic dimension of the whole. The robust and imposing plasticity of the architecture adds to the sober stateliness of this area. The facade of Palazzo Senatorio was adapted from the Michelangelesque plan by Giacomo Della Porta and Girolamo Rainaldi, with its entrance facing the piazza, characteristic double flights of steps, stucco facing and row of gigantic Corinthian pilasters strips. The balustrade looking out over the city, with its monumental *Dioscuri*, was also conceived to complement the piazza, and was modified by Della Porta in 1585.

24

Virgin in Benediction
Santa Maria in Aracoeli

The icon is inserted in the centre of the altarpiece in the main chapel of the Church of Santa Maria in Aracoeli. According to popular tradition the sacred image was amongst those attributed to Saint Luke. The tablet portrays Mary with the «palla» (ball), decorated with a border and little gold crosses, and with her hand raised in an attitude of prayer. It is an iconographic copy, executed with a very forceful and incisive style in the middle of the XIth century. The painting is in translucent colours, similar to enamel, and is reminiscent of oriental workmanship.

It is one of the images most revered by Romans, and, among the numerous votive offerings dedicated to it, by far the most significant is the big flight of steps of 1348. There are numerous replicas of this prototype, where the Virgin is presented as mediator between Christ and the faithful. The icon was originally found in the tabernacle, which was commissioned by the antipope Anacletus II and built on the site of the present Cappella of Sant'Elena. It was Pius IV who placed it on the main altar, where the Madonna of Foligno painted by Raphael in 1511-1512 had been until 1565.

25

Musei Capitolini

The Capitoline Museum, the oldest museum collection of antiquity, was built at the behest of Pope Sixtus IV, who, in 1471, gave the Roman people four famous bronze statues (the Capitoline Wolf, the Spinario, the Camillo and the head of Constantine with the hand and the globe) which had hitherto been kept in front of the Lateran Patriarchìo as a symbol of the continuity between Imperial Rome and the Church. With the construction of the Palazzo Nuovo, commissioned by Clement VIII in 1603, most of the works hoarded in the Palazzo dei Conservatori could be accommodated. In 1734 the Capitoline Museum was opened to the public after Pope Clement XII arranged for the acquisition of the collection of statues and portraits belonging to Cardinal Albani. In the middle of the XVIIIth century Pope Benedict XIV founded the Pinacoteca Capitolina which was rich in paintings from private collections. After numerous urban excavations organised at the end of 1800 to celebrate Rome as capital city, huge quantities of material flowed in to the museum and new exhibition centres were set up, including the Capitoline Medal Collection. Between 1925 and 1930 the Museo Mussolini, which became the Museo Nuovo, was founded after the acquisition of Palazzo Caffarelli. In 1956 the Palazzo dei Conservatori was enlarged with the construction of the Braccio Nuovo, where important sculptures from Republican Rome were exhibited.

Renovation work in the Capitoline Museum has brought about the creation of other decentralised branches. The reorganisation of exhibition space allocated to the Capitoline Museum complex has led to the Tabularium being opened to the public. This is connected to the other buildings by the Galleria di Congiunzione and the new wing of the Palazzo dei Conservatori.

Caravaggio, The Fortune Teller.

Mosaic of the Doves, second century BC, and Capitoline Wolf, fifth century BC.

Spinario
Musei Capitolini

The bronze statue, which portrays a seated boy in the act of removing a thorn from his foot, belonged to the imperial collections which were donated to the Bishop of Rome during the Constantinian age and given back to the Roman people by Sixtus IV in 1471, together with other Lateran bronzes. There are various interpretations of the work, which is among the most prized and celebrated from the Middle Ages to the modern age. Some believe that it is an eclectic work from the first century BC, the body being based on Hellenistic models of the third to the second century BC, and the head on a prototype from the Vth centruy BC. Others posit the hypothesis of an arbitrary montage of two originals in late antiquity, the figure being created in an Asian context in about 120 BC and the head, having previously belonged to a statue of Eros, being identified with the style of Severus (Vth century BC).

Marcus Aurelius
Musei Capitolini

The famous bronze work portrays Marcus
Aurelius on horseback and was originally
probably part of a triumphal monument;
recent hypotheses are based on the
theory that in antiquity the colossus
formed part of an equestrian group,
together with a statue of the daughter of
the Emperor Commodus. A no longer
young Marcus Aurelius gestures with his
right hand to emphasise his wish for a
peacemaking act in line with the
philosophical ideals expressed in the
Memories, his spiritual diary. The
monument was probably erected on the
occasion of his death in 180 AD. It
escaped being melted down because in
the Middle Ages it was thought to
represent Constantine, the first Christian
Emperor, in the act of benediction. The
statue was moved from the Lateran
Palazzo to the Campidoglio in 1536 at the
wish of Pope Paul III Farnese, who
employed Michelangelo to install Marcus
Aurelius in the middle of the piazza. The
original, which has been moved inside the
museum, has been replaced by a faithful
copy.

Piazza Venezia

In 1466 Paul II moved two huge Terme di Caracalla granite basins from the original platea nova to Piazza Farnese. Thus the reigning pontiff implemented the first phase in the evolution of Piazza Venezia, which, as the monumental figurehead of the Corso, was taking shape in relation to the gradual building of Palazzo Venezia,. It represented the first big urban change in Renaissance Rome and became the theatrical arrival point of the famous race of the Bàrberi which, in carnival season, started in Piazza del Popolo and wound its way along the Corso with a festive crowd and the richest nobility looking on. A dense urban network of medieval origin linked it to the Capitoline Hill and an area of crowded fifteenth and sixteenth buildings joined it to the Monti rione beyond the Imperial Forums. When the decision was taken in 1882 to erect the monument to Vittorio Emanuele II as a backdrop to the Corso, in the lee of the Campidoglio, substantial changes had to be made to the whole area, which had hitherto ended in the piazza. In 1845 the latter had witnessed the first appearance of a horse omnibus and gas lighting. The next step was the demolition of the buildings sheltered by the monument; this enlarged the piazza, which was extended even further after the demolition of the sixteenth century Palazzo Torlonia, opposite Palazzo Venezia. Next the Assicurazioni Generali building was constructed, in the style of

the Pauline complex; this was placed further back in the piazza. Palazzo Venezia, which had already been commissioned by Cardinal Pietro Barbo as a prestigious private residence in about 1464, was subjected to considerable changes when Paul II was elected pontiff, to make it fit for a «papal palace». As a residence of the ambassadors of the Venetian Republic in 1564, the palazzo underwent further changes when it passed first of all to the Hapsburg Empire and then, in the Napoleonic period, to the Italic Kingdom, when it became home to the Accademia di Belle Arti directed by Antonio Canova. It was to undergo further changes when, between 1929 and 1943, it was home to the head of government and

the Great Council of fascism. Meanwhile the outlook of the piazza had evolved in 1911 with the inauguration of the central Monument and the definitive layout of the area. When the axes of Via del Mare and Via dei Fori Imperiali were opened during the twenty years of fascism, the piazza, which was proclaimed the Forum of Italy, was confirmed in its role as both symbolic and geographical centre of the city.

Left, Palazzo Venezia. Right, view of Piazza Venezia.

Following pages: Giuseppe Sacconi, *Monument to the Unknown Soldier.*

29

The Gesù

The Gesù Church is an extremely important example of late sixteenth century religious architecture and it played a fundamental role in further developments in Rome's sacred architecture in the seventeenth century. The complex history of the church begins in 1537, with the arrival in Rome after an absence of fourteen years of Saint Ignatius of Loyola. He personally chose the place where the mother church of the Order, the Company of Jesus, of which he was the founder, was to be built. It was recognised by Paul III in 1540 and destined to become one of the most powerful of the Counter-Reformation. But many years passed before the scheme for the building was carried out; it needed the economic power of a character like Cardinal Alessandro Farnese, the nephew of Pope Paul III, to drive the building project forward. At the time of its dedication in 1584, the church was the biggest and first completely new one built since the Sack of Rome in 1527. The Gesù Church is also known as the Farnesian Temple. The saying went that Cardinal Farnese possessed the three most beautiful things in Rome: his family palazzo, his daughter Clelia and the Gesù Church. The novelty of the temple conceived by the architect Domenico Vignola is evident above all in the blueprint. The Gesù was the prototype for a kind of temple with a single hall, which was adapted to the liturgical and devotional demands of the Counter-Reformation and Jesuitical preaching in particular.

Two Jesuit architects participated in the design of the volumetric plan of the building, which has a very compressed

transept with three side chapels, and is the result of the fusion of the central plan favoured in the Renaissance and the longitudinal one of the ancient Christian tradition. Then, at the end of the XVIIth century, the temple would be transformed into one of the finest examples of European Baroque, by the wonderful

trompe l'oeuil painting of Giovan Battista Gaulli, or 'Baciccio', as he was known.

Andrea Pozzo, *Saint Ignatius Altar.*

30

Adoration of the Name of Jesus
Gesù Church ceiling

On the 21st of August in 1672 the Genovese Giovan Battista Gaulli, or 'Baciccia', signed a contract with the Company of Gesù for the frescoes and gilding of the ceiling of the nave, the dome, the pendentives and the ceiling of the transept of the Gesù Church. Gaulli, who was born in 1639, had already made his name as a portraitist, although he had done very little decorative work. That the Jesuits, the most powerful religious order in Rome, had very little faith in the young artist is obvious from the contract they made him sign. In effect the painter had to paint the huge interior space of the church at his own expense; it had to be finished by 1682; in addition the decoration had to be judged by a committee of experts, and, if fault was found, Gaulli had to agree to remedy the mistakes without pay. The feat accomplished by Baciccia, in much less time, surpassed all expectations. Today it is unanimously considered the masterpiece of the Genovese artist, with the brilliantly illusionistic movement of the swirling, vertiginous throng which seems to emerge from the frame to create a synthesis of painting, sculpture and architecture, the very symbol of great Baroque decoration. On the ceiling, he painted the Adoration of the Name of Jesus, an expression, on a grand scale, of the essential characteristic of Jesuit propaganda: the glorification of its missionary role. Gaulli found inspiration for the theme in the daring, revolutionary fresco which Pietro da Cortona had painted in Palazzo Barberini. The whole composition revolves around the luminous circle containing the emblem of the Company (IHS), which is placed at the centre of the ceiling. A blinding light bathes the ranks of saints and the blessed and strikes the damned and the heretics. A remarkable trompe l'oeuil effect makes it seem as if these are falling out of the painting's frame, past the stucco decoration of the ceiling to plunge into the church below. The bright, warm colours and the contrast between the brown, blue and red tones of the figures, with their heightened chiaroscuro, on the one hand, and the dazzling light of the Name of Jesus on the other, create an overall effect of cosmic drama. Apart from the faithful, there are sixteen onlookers at this terrible scene, made out of stucco and placed in the window recesses along the nave. With their transfixed and fearful expressions they at once belong to the drama and intensify it, as well as symbolising the Jesuit missionary activity as personifications of all the regions, from Ethiopia to Peru, and from China to Mexico.

31

Giovanni Lanfranco, Frescoes in Sant'Andrea della Valle

A pupil of Agostino Carracci, Giovanni Lanfranco had moved to Rome in 1602. It was the period spent in Parma between 1610 and 1612 which brought about a substantial change in the painter's style, thanks to his re-appraisal of the works of Correggio. This enabled him to enrich his painting considerably, attaining an unusual naturalistic facility and heightened dynamism. This is the background for the decoration of the dome of Sant'Andrea della Valle whose splendid trompe l'oeuil effects and originality had a decisive influence on the development of Baroque decorative painting. He had been summoned to decorate the dome of the mother church of the Theatine Order in1621. At the behest of Costanza Piccolomini d'Aragona, it had been begun in1591 and finished by Carlo Maderno in the first half of the 17th century. While the classical Bolognese painter Domenichino decorated the bowl-shaped apse and pendentives of the dome with frescoes, Giovanni Lanfranco created a complex and exuberant decorative scheme. There is a freedom and dynamism about the composition of the figures within the space, due to the absence of any sort of architectural framework, and the bodies have a sculptural quality, derived from

Annibale Carracci, and a particularly delicate chromatic range. The painter was engaged on the cycle of frescoes from1621 to 1627 and it is an essential point of reference in terms of large trompe l'oeil decoration, as, thanks to the skilful use of luminous tones and chiaroscuro, it implies continuity between real and painted space. The figures are depicted in a particularly naturalistic manner and seem to float in the cloud-filled air. The focal point of the composition, which has been conceived with a precise and constructive harmony, is the figure of the Virgin. She is placed in the centre, surrounded by an exultant group of the Blessed, Saints, and Cherubs with mischievous expressions, as well as Angels playing music. The figures occupy the space in the form of a spiral. Crowned with garlands and rings of cherubs, they seem to be caught in a descending vortex, which begins in the lantern and brims over onto the octagonal walls, up to the windows at the top. The airy, festive spirit is a precursor of the vertiginous feats of more mature baroque decorations.

Museo Barracco

The small palazzo which is the present home of the Museo Barracco was built in about 1523, probably from the design of Antonio da Sangallo il Giovane. The building is also known as «Farnesina ai Baullari» due to the erroneous attribution to the Farnese of the building's characteristic decorative element, the lily, which is actually part of the coat of arms of the patron, the Breton, Le Roy. The building, which had already been restored after the Sack of Rome in 1527, has been subject to considerable change in the course of time, especially after the expropriations necessitated by the opening of Corso Vittorio Emanuele. The demolition and subsequent rebuilding, carried out under the architect Guy at the end of the 19th century, have drastically changed the original appearance of the palazzo, which can only be appreciated in the facade in

Via dell'Aquila. Since1948, the building has housed the splendid collection of Sumerian, Assyrian, Egyptian, Greek, Etruscan and Roman art, donated in 1902 by Giovanni Barracco to the Comune di Roma. At the time, the collector undertook, at his own expense, to construct an elegant building, designed by the architect Gaetano Koch, in Corso Vittorio Emanuele. It was demolished in 1938, in line with the demands of the new regulating plan. The sculptures were then moved to the Capitoline Museum store until 1947, when the collection found its new home in the Le Roy palazzo. The collection of sculptures, numbering about 380, was gradually built up by Barracco, buying directly from excavations and antique dealers. It contains many pieces which serve to illustrate the history of antique art. The exhibition is divided into themed rooms in

chronological order, from the Egyptian to the late Imperial ages. On the first floor, in order, are Egyptian, Sumerian, Assyrian, Etruscan and Cypriot sculptures, and on the second floor there are Greek, Roman and medieval works. The Roman age copies of famous Greek originals are particularly important: the head of the Apollo Liceo, the Lisippus Wounded Bitch, the Myron Marsyas, the Doriforo and Diadumeno heads by Policletus and the Apollo Kassel.

Relief of noble ladies examining material.

Head of priest or Julius Caesar. Next page: funerary relief.

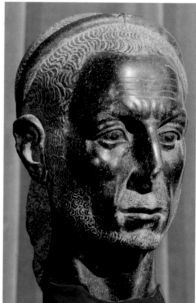

33

Annibale Carracci, Landscape with the Flight into Egypt
Galleria Doria Pamphilj

The Landscape with the Flight into Egypt is one of the six lunettes with Stories of the Virgin which decorated the chapel of Cardinal Pietro Aldobrandini in the Palazzo al Corso. The commission was probably entrusted to Annibale in about 1603, but it took a long time to complete. As the health of the master gradually deteriorated, the lunettes were finished by other pupils, under the guidance of Francesco Albani. From the end of the VIIth century, the Flight into Egypt was, to all effects, considered a landscape. In this period «landscapes» invaded entrance halls, galleries and the studies of palazzi, with preference given to the Flemish ones. However, something new happens on the walls of Pietro's chapel and, in particular, with the Flight into Egypt. In this work Annibale intoduces an original concept of landscape which was to become a

watershed in the history of European classical culture. Noble idealism and natural detail fuse to form a perfect creation of the «ideal» landscape, a long way from the descriptivism of Flemish painting. The effect sought is that of the perfect sentimental harmony of sacred characters, their history and the surrounding landscape. This is idealised for the purpose, although it remains true to life in terms of light, colour and atmospheric effects. The placing of buildings in the distance in order to balance the composition has been carefully thought out. The animals represented contribute to the authenticity of the historical narration, as in the case of the camels on the horizon; they are barely suggested and almost transparent. Thus the outline of the trees on the left in the half shadow is emphasised by use of back

lighting and this draws attention to the pond, its surroundings and the landscape beyond. Their presence is perfectly balanced by the two trees in the background on the right. It is a new formula, at the same time calm and meditative, classical and natural, for the context of the holy story. The simplicity and quest for clarity in the expression of the emotions of Renaissance painting is still there; the objective is to recreate the cultured beauty of the antique, perfect nature, with a tranquil horizon and sweeping views towards the background, light blue spaces and infinite clear light.

34

Filippino Lippi, frescoes in the Cappella Carafa Santa Maria sopra Minerva

In 1488, Filippino Lippi, thanks to the mediation of Lorenzo il Magnifico, was called to Rome to decorate the Chapel of Cardinal Oliviero Carafa in Santa Maria sopra Minerva with frescoes. At the time, he was occupied with the decoration of the Chapel of Filippo Strozzi in Santa Maria Novella in Florence and the stay in Rome gave him the opportunity to broaden his knowledge of the antique, with «in-depth study, above all of vases, footwear, trophies, flags, helmets, temple ornaments, head-dresses, strange-shaped hoods, armour, scimitars, swords, togas, cloaks and other diverse and beautiful things», as Giorgio Vasari writes in 1568.

The painter referred to as «nuovo Apelles» by the cultured Cardinal Carafa in a letter of 1488 and as the artist «of such graceful inventions», as Vasari put it, worked speedily on the project, giving it precedence over the Strozzi Chapel and probably finishing it as early as September 1489. The humanistic and theological scheme for the chapel clearly alludes to papal supremacy. Cultured allegory and fairy-tale narration are combined. The artist exploits the classical architectural frameworks and backgrounds imaginatively, embellishing them with liberal grotesque decoration and a rich repertoire of archeological motifs: festoons, friezes and heroic figures adorn and prevail over the architectural settings. There are, however, cases where the accuracy in reference to the antique reveals an attentive study of classicism, including the phililogical aspect, on the artist's part, for instance, in the scene of the Triumph of Saint Thomas, where in the background Filippino has painted a delicate view of Rome with the statue of Marcus Aurelius in front of the Lateran. There is an elegant trompe l'oeuil style and particular narrative sensibility about the scene of the Annunciation, which is presented as a pretence panel inserted in the fresco decoration and surrounded by an elegant stucco frame.

35

Pantheon

The Pantheon is stituated in the Roman Regio (quarter) IX, corresponding to Campus Martius. According to legend, Campus Martius used to belong to the Tarquins and was a marshy area. When the last Etruscan king was expelled from Rome in 509 BC, the year the Republic was founded, the area became public. Augustus began filling the central area of Campus Martius with monuments and rebuilding the buildings in the Circus Flaminius area. The temple – dedicated to all the gods – was intended to be a symbol of the Emperor Augustus and therefore of his family, the gens Iulia. The present appearance of the Pantheon is owed to its rebuilding by Hadrian between 118 and 125 AD. This maintained the blueprint of the previous construction, except where the level of the base was raised and the width of the pronaos reduced to eight columns. The inscription on the architrave referring to the building of the temple by Agrippa was retained by Hadrian, who never had his name inscribed on any of the monuments he built, with the exception of Trajan's temple. A second inscription in smaller letters records the restoration by Septimius Severus and Caracalla in 202 AD. In 609 AD the Byzantine Emperor Foca gave the Pantheon to Pope Boniface IV, and so the temple was changed into the Chiesa di Santa Maria ad Martyres. A flight of steps led up to a large portico with eight monolithic granite columns with white marble capitals and bases. Two more rows of four columns formed the three aisles. The monumental bronze door is probably original, although it is has been restored many times. The dome is the largest one built prior to the twentieth century; it measures 43,30 metres in diameter and was built using a huge wooden framework. The use of layers of concrete alternated with tufa and pumice served to lessen the weight of the huge structure. The height of the temple from the floor to the top of the dome is equal to the diameter of the latter, meaning that a sphere could fit into the interior, so that there is a perfect balance in the building's proportions. On the inside the dome is adorned with five rows of coffering which were probably originally decorated with gilded bronze elements.

Andrea Pozzo, Glory of Saint Ignatius
Sant'Ignazio

When the general Oliva called the thirty-eight year old Andrea Pozzo to Rome in 1680, the Chiesa di Sant'Ignazio, which had been open since 1642, still had a bare and unornamented appearance. Pozzo, who was born in Trento, was a Jesuit and had made his reputation in northern Italy decorating several of the order's churches with impressive effects in terms of perspective. When he arrived in Rome he devoted himself to the decoration of the church, painting the series of stories of the saint and the Company of Jesus in the corridor of the convent annexe, the pretence dome with projecting architectural motifs (a large flat canvas with painted perspective effects, creating the illusion of an authentic dome, noted at the time as «rather vague and artificial»), the pendentives with their biblical figures, the choir and, lastly, the spectacular nave ceiling. This seems pierced by very sharply fore-shortened architectural features which

open out in the centre with the portrayal of the titular saint in glory. The ceiling decoration project began in 1688 and, in this case as well, it was used as a means of celebrating the Jesuits' missionary

activity. The light comes from God the Father to the Son, who transmits it to Saint Ignatius, and it splits into four rays leading to the four continents. The figurative and architectural elements merge and the illusionistic details are resolved by the juxtaposition of blinding rays of light and areas of shadow, in a manner reminiscent of Gaulli. The trompe l'oeuil perspectives of Pozzo, whether in the paintings of the dome, the apse or the Saint Ignatius ceiling, constitute one of the most remarkable legacies of Baroque Rome. With his perspective and the idea of using pretence architecture to expand space, Pozzo also provided an example which was later followed in many Italian, Austrian and German churches of the Jesuit order.

Left, Andrea Pozzo, *Allegory of Africa*, and top, *Allegory of Asia*.

Right, Andrea Pozzo, *Entry of Saint Ignatius into Paradise*.

37

Piazza Navona

Thanks to its original elongated form, Piazza Navona deserves a foremost place among Rome's numerous historical piazzas. Built on the site of the former Domitian stadium, it traditionally accommodated the market and popular shows. During the XVIIth century it became the city's salon, partly because of the presence of Palazzo Pamphilj, and it was embellished with further monuments and buildings. These enhance the spatial homogeneity which is owed to the regularity of the architectural features packed into the unbroken ranks of walls and facades, and to the chromatic unity. A result of the urban plans for the piazza under the patronage of Innocent X Pamphilj, who was responsible for the complete reorganisation of the area and the demolition of some blocks, was the concave facade of Sant'Agnese. The work of Borromini, it merges with the walls surrounding the piazza, copying the essential architectural motifs and presenting an emblematic example of dynamic integration between the building and the space in front of it, which acts as an extension to the church and seems to disappear into it. In the layout of the piazza, a role of no lesser importance is played by the three fountains which serve to break up the huge horizontal space into four distinct areas. The focus is the symbolic and actual centre of the *Fontana dei Quattro Fiumi*, the work of Gian Lorenzo Bernini. It is a spectacular allegory of the worldly prestige of the Pamphilj: an aerial «natural grotto». The four springs of faraway rivers spout from it and it is studded with exotic plants and animals. It acts as a base for the Egyptian obelisk crowned with a dove, the symbol of the Pamphilj and the Holy Spirit.

Fontana dei Quattro Fiumi.

38

Caravaggio, Stories of Saint Matthew
San Luigi dei Francesi

Thanks to the mediation of Cardinal Del Monte from the July of 1599 to that of 1600, Caravaggio painted the two side canvases for the Chapel of Cardinal Contarelli in San Luigi dei Francesi, his first public commission. The Calling and Martyrdom of Saint Matthew were both demanding in terms of the depiction of a story in action and the numerous figures. The symbolic role of the light, coupled with the natural illumination of the chapel, lends unity to the whole. With these canvases

Caravaggio brings contemporary reality into a sacred scene and into a church chapel for the first time. Characters dressed in the current style participate in the sacred event as they go about their daily life, intent on tavern games. The first canvas to be finished was the Calling. Caravaggio constructs the scene around the gesture of Christ, who points towards Matthew and whose hand position is mirrored by the latter's. The two groups are unified by the shaft of light, whose origin is

outside the field of vision, above the head of Jesus. The light is both divine and natural and also serves as an efficacious stylistic expedient to emphasise the evident contrast between the modern clothes of Matthew and his companions and the few divine attributes of the apostle, who is barefoot and wrapped in a large cloak of antique style. In the case of the Martyrdom, the focal point of the scene is the executioner, who is in the act of striking the martyr. The other characters

are placed around the central figure, gradually going further back into the bare space which is the scene of the action. Caravaggio freezes the dramatic moment before the death by means of the light. This is concentrated on the naked body of the executioner poised to strike and on the angel who proffers the palm of martyrdom to the saint.

Once it was placed on the altar of the chapel, the altar-piece of Saint Matthew and the Angel, which was done in three and a half months in 1602, was, according to Bellori: «taken away by the priests, who said that the figure had neither the decorum nor appearance of a saint, with

his legs apart and his feet roughly exposed to the people». In fact the image of the saint as an illiterate who seemed to be receiving help with his reading from the angel was too much for the people. So Caravaggio replaced the canvas with a new version which was more in line with the tastes of the priesthood: the saint is no longer a peasant; he emanates wisdom while the angel flies down towards his shoulders.

Caravaggio, *Calling of Saint Matthew.*

Caravaggio, *Martyrdom of Saint Matthew.*

Palazzo Altemps

The elegant palazzo was built between the end of the XVth and XVIth centuries. After the faithful and praiseworthy restoration by the Archeological Service, it now houses some of the antiquities acquired by its former owner, Cardinal Marco Altemps, and numerous works belonging to other fine Roman collections, all displayed in the fresco-decorated rooms in a novel and refreshing way. The sculptures come from the Mattei collection in Villa Celimontana, from the Del Drago collection and from the seventeenth century Boncompagni-Ludovisi collection. The masterpieces of the latter were restored by prominent baroque artists such as, Gian Lorenzo Bernini and Alessandro Algardi (the Discus Thrower, Acrolith, Ludovisi Throne, Ares, Juno, Erinyes and the Ludovisi sarcophogus, and the Galatian and his wife committing suicide). Also of great interest are the Egyptian sculptures found in the Santuario di Iside in Campus Martius and the sumptuous Chiesa di Sant Aniceto, built in the grounds by Giovanni Angelo Altemps between 1603 and 1618 with frescoes by Pomarancio.

View of the fresco-decorated loggia.

Ludovisi Throne
Museo di Palazzo Altemps

The relief known as the Ludovisi Throne was only found as recently as 1887 in the area of the Horti Sallustiani, and at the time of its discovery it was thought to be the back of a colossal cult statue. The marble relief by Thasos is in an unusual tryptich form made up of three sculpted slabs. On the sides are depictions of female figures seated in profile; one is dressed in a cloak and veil and is in the act of throwing incense on an incense-burner, and one, a nude, is playing the double flute. The goddess, depicted half-length on the front wearing a chiton and supported by two handmaidens who are holding a veil over the lower half of her body, is thought by most to be Aphrodite being born from the sea. Scholars continue to be puzzled by the unusual form and scene and there have been doubts as to the authenticity of the work. For stylistic reasons the relief has been dated around 460-450 BC and its origin attributed to Magna Grecia. Current opinion places it as a work of the Greek colony of Locri Epizefiri, and as an element of the sacred furnishing of a temple of Aphrodite.

The Galatian and his wife committing suicide
Museo di Palazzo Altemps

Many of the works which make up the Ludovisi collection were found in the area where the family villa was built, which had also been the site of a rich residence in antiquity, belonging first to Caesar, then to his friend the writer Sallust and finally reverting to imperial ownership. Among the works discovered was the famous scuptural group of the Galatian warrior who kills himself and his wife in order not to fall into the enemy's hands. The bronze original reproduced from the Roman copy was part of a gift to the Gods executed by the scuptor Epigonos in about 230 BC, in celebration of the victory of the King of Pergamum, Attalo, over the Galatians (the Celts of Asia Minor). The group must have been at the centre of a circular base and had other defeated barbarians around it, like the dying Galatian now in the Palatine Museum. The provenance of both of these sculptures lends weight to the hypothesis that Caesar had these copies made to celebrate his victory over the Gauls, the Western equivalent of the Galatians. Impressive features of this masterpiece of Hellenistic Pergamum art are its pyramidal composition, with its opposed axes, the characters' ethnic characteristics, the powerful muscles of the Galatian, and the involvement in the sculpture's space of the spectator, who empathises and shares in the destiny of the defeated partly because they command respect.

Caravaggio, Madonna dei Pellegrini
Sant'Agostino

She is a woman of the people, with her baby in her arms, looking out of the door of her house, an ordinary Roman house, and welcoming the two wayfarers with dirty, bare feet and patched clothes. With their pilgrim staffs and hands together, the two kneel in the presence of the woman, so physically close to them, yet so far in the palpable sacred dimension which envelops them. Baglione relates that in about 1620, when the painting was placed in the Cappella di Ermete Cavalletti in the Chiesa di Sant'Agostino, the people were shocked. The problem was that, once again, Caravaggio had taken the representation of the real to extremes to express the very essence of the religious dimension. In the languid pose and the realism of the skin tones of that Madonna the Romans had immediately recognised the model who had posed for the artist with her baby. Maddalena Antognetti, who was known as Lena, was a well-known figure in the city; she had been the lover of many powerful men and her life as a courtesan had recently also got her into trouble with the law. Another reason for the public outrage, besides more uplifting religious questions, must have been the difficulty posed by the idea of gathering in prayer before a figure who could hardly have been further from embodying the essence of spirituality. On the other hand, apart from the sophisticated adherence to the truth, which had also led Caravaggio to place the dirty feet of the pilgrims in the foreground, the painting was also partly based on a composition taken from the much admired Titian. The great Venetian was also the source of the velvety red flesh tones of the Madonna. These subtle references would not have counted for much with the common people and it was equally difficult to tell that the pose, and in fact the profile of the Madonna, were taken from classical statuary.

43

Fontana di Trevi

The Fontana di Trevi, a happy and successful marriage of classicism and baroque, was planned as an exhibition of the Acqua Vergine by Nicola Salvi under the patronage of Clement XII. Pope Urban VIII Barberini had already instructed Gian Lorenzo Bernini to «transform» the piazza and the fountain, but the project was never carried out. Set along one side of Palazzo Poli, the fountain, which was made by Nicola Salvi between 1732 and 1763, represents an original and imaginative fusion, in the Berninian style, of architecture, sculpture and the natural elements which contribute to the fountain's unique character. The theme of the sculpture is the sea. The design is dominated by a chariot in the form of a shell in which the great statue of Neptune by Pietro Bracci stands, flanked in the side niches by Health and Plenty, the works of Filippo Della Valle. The chariot is pulled by marine horses, who are in turn preceded by tritons. The marine divinities are placed on rocks of irregular blocks of travertine. The fountain sprawls below the facade of the palazzo behind it, which is in rigidly classicising style, based on the triumphal arch model, with further sculptures in niches as well as in the attic storey and an elegant balustrade. The surrounding houses crowd round the splendid monument, giving the impression of an amphitheatre, while the noise of the fountain's water can be heard from the maze of surrounding streets up to the moment when the snow-white scene appears miraculously before the astonished eyes of the visitor.

44

Palazzo Barberini

The rise of the Barberini, one of the most powerful of the Roman Papal families, is closely connected to the ecclesiastical career of Cardinal Maffeo Barberini, the future Pope, who was elected with the name Urban VIII in 1623. The family's prestige in the papal city was from that moment secured and culminated in the construction in the grand style of the palazzo, which was to become one of the most admired in Rome at the time. Some of the main artists of the age were involved in the building and decoration of the prestigious residence: Carlo Maderno, Gian Lorenzo Bernini and Francesco Borromini sought to outdo each other in a contest of elegance, as did Pietro da Cortona and Andrea Sacchi in their paintings for the palazzo. Everything, from the architecture to the magnificence of the

frescoes and interior furnishings had to reflect the authority and affluence of the line who had chosen this way of leaving an indelible mark on the heart of the city. In 1629, the year in which Maderno died, the palazzo had however only just been begun, so the building was then entrusted to Gian Lorenzo Bernini, the official artist par excellence of the Barberinian court. He saw the construction through, collaborating at first with Francesco Borromini, in whose hands, according to Baldinucci, Maderno had left «the entire care of the palazzo» and who, still in the words of the biographer did «all the designs for the said building». One of the most elaborate residences of Baroque Rome, and a refined theatre for the sumptuous feasts organised by the family, grew from the meeting of these three masters. For instance, on the evening of the 28th of February 1656, the Cavallerizza courtyard, on the North side of the building and now part of Via Barberini, was host to a marvellous entertainment given in honour of Cristina of Sweden: a colourful merry-go-round with an elegant parade of carriages and ephemeral displays devised by Giovan Francesco Grimaldi, the family scenographer, and a festive throng drawn from the most prestigious nobility. The reception hall in Palazzo Barberini was decorated between 1633 and 1639 with the splendid fresco painted on the vaulted ceiling by Pietro da Cortona, on an allegorical theme extolling the glory of the papal family and elaborated by the poet Francesco Bracciolini. In the vast hall, which is in fact a huge empty space, the symmetrical forms break away from the traditional system of divisions and frames

used by Annibale Carrracci in the Galleria Farnese, to vie with one another in dissolving the boundary between real and painted space in a spectacular new harmony. The impression of magnification is created by the false trabeations framing an open sky. This is animated by scenes symbolising good government and the virtues of the pope and his family. The illusionistic effect is complemented by monochrome clipei at the corners, depicting scenes from Roman history relevant to virtue.

Grand staircase with doric columns and spiral staircase.

45

Trinità dei Monti and Piazza di Spagna

The Villa Medici and its big park were created at the end of the XVIth century where, in antiquity, there had been the gardens of Lucullus, who was celebrated in Latin literature for his passion for gastronomy and the art of living. Cardinal Ricci acquired the land in 1564, had a palazzo built on it by the Florentine architect Nanni di Baccio Bigio and was responsible for the first significant phase of works. In 1576 Cardinal Ferdinando de' Medici, the great collector and patron, bought the estate and entrusted the Florentine architect Bartolomeo Ammannati with a very ambitious project. Ferdinando de' Medici, a lover of antiquity, conceived the villa as a museum, with a refined gallery-antiquarium. The garden was also planned in a theatrical spirit, on the lines of botanical gardens created by the Medici family in Pisa and Florence. Many rare plants were to be found in it, together with numerous antiquities. The palazzo was only to recover its status as a haven for the arts in the XIXth century, when it became the seat of the Académie Française in Rome. Below the villa is the expanse of one of the most picturesque piazzas in Rome, with the theatrical backdrop of the monumental XIIIth century flight of steps of Trintità dei Monti leading down to the distinctive Barcaccia fountain, which was the work of Pietro Bernini in 1629. The Piazza di Spagna, which forms a splendid background to the Via dei Condiotti and is a real "icon" of the city, is one of the most monumental and theatrical urban complexes in Rome. From the XVIth century onwards, the space between it and the nearby Via Margutta and Via Babuino was a meeting point for artists and writers, and the area was animated by antique shops, inns and elegant residential buildings. However it was between the seventeenth and eighteenth centuries that the piazza took on its present appearance, with the distinctive 'butterfly' shape, formed by two triangles with a common vertex. Having initially been called 'alla Trinità', after the church which dominates it, it came to be known as the Piazza di Spagna in reference to the Spanish ambassador's residence there. 1629 was the year in which Pietro Bernini and his son Gian Lorenzo executed the Barcaccia fountain. This was conceived to commemorate the flooding of the Tiber in 1598, and its distinctive boat shape is an allusion to the Church being under the safe guidance of the Barberini. It rests on the ground inside another elliptical-shaped basin, which acts as the spatial pivot of the piazza, but it is the central steps which make this one of the most famous settings of the city. Built by Francesco De Sanctis between 1723 and 1726 under the patronage of Innocent XIII, to resolve the difference in level between the Chiesa di Trinità dei Monti and the piazza below, the Spanish steps are based on the design of the port of Ripetta sul Tevere, which was built in 1704 by Alessandro Specchi and then destroyed. The daring solution is a confirmation of the theatrical bent of late-Baroque urban planning in the capital. It includes impressive balustraded terraces embraced by two wings of steps, which, in an elegant fan motif and alternating and curvilenear movement of converging and diverging ramps, merge to flow down into the piazza below.

46

Ara Pacis

To celebrate the victorious return of Augustus from military campaigns in Spain and Gaul, in 13 BC the Senate voted for the construction of a monumental altar for the Augustan Peace, which was dedicated in 9BC. The monument was built to the west of the Via Flaminia, in the northern part of Campus Martius, an area which was radically remodelled by the Augustan changes. The altar itself was surrounded by a rectangular marble screen, with reliefs sculpted in two sections. On the inside, the upper area is decorated with festoons and sacrificial goblets, while the lower one reproduces in marble the posts of the wooden fence which had originally enclosed the sacred area. On the outside, the slabs of the lower section are covered with extremely elegant acanthus volutes, while in the upper reliefs there are figurative scenes, illustrating fundamental themes of Augustan policy in the style of Greek art of the Classical and Hellenistic age. In the panels on the short sides, where the two entrances are, there are representations of mythological scenes connected to the foundation of Rome and the traditional religion, which Augustus wished to extol. On one side is the grotto known as Lupercalia, where the wolf suckled Romulus and Remus, and the sacrifice of Aeneas to the Penates; on the other are personifications of the Earth flourishing thanks to the peace, and of Rome, triumphant under the rule of Augustus. On the long sides is a religious procession, among the participants Augustus, Livia, Agrippa, who had died in 12 BC, and all the members of the imperial family in hierarchical order can be recognised. The position of each was determined by their relationship to the prince and role in the line of succession. The frieze of the interior altar, which is crowned with volutes, depicts the canonical sacrifice of the three victims - the pig, the sheep and the bull- which was performed annually in the presence of the Vestal virgins and the most important priests, in a style which is closer to the Roman-Italic tradition.

Tellus and above, Detail of the *Procession of Agrippa*

Piazza del Popolo and Santa Maria del Popolo

«You are a world, Rome!» Goethe exclaimed, as soon as he had entered the city by the Porta del Popolo, and, after days of walking, found himself in the harmonious piazza. The huge space, which is closed to the north by the gate of the same name and dominated to the east by the ramp of the Pincio walkway, and is so wisely orchestrated from the point of view of town-planning, architecture,

landscaping and urban decoration, evolved in the space of three and a half centuries. Since Medieval times, the church of Santa Maria del Popolo had welcomed the traveller and pilgrim who arrived in the city, weary after days of walking, by the Via Flaminia. It started off as a mere chapel built from the funds of the Roman people; then, in the XIIIth century Gregory IX enlarged it and in 1250 it underwent

further changes when it passed to the Augustinians. However, in the XVth century, from 1472 onwards to be exact, during the pontificate of Sixtus IV, to mark the occasion of the 1475 Jubilee, the Lombard congregation commissioned its rebuilding in accordance with the canons of contemporary sacred Lombard architecture. Later, significant alterations were made by Bramante, Raphael and

Bernini. The decorative and sculptural array with which the church was embellished during the XVI century therefore make it one of the most complete of the Roman churches in terms of examples of the art of the time. The masterpieces left here by some of the most important artists active in Rome from the XVIth to the XVIIth century, from Andrea Sansovino to Bernini, from Caravaggio to Annibale Carracci and Carlo Maratta, create on of the most precious treasure troves of works of art in the city. It was on the occasion of the arrival in Rome of Queen Cristina of Sweden that the area took on its baroque form. Then Alexander VII Chigi renovated the piazza under the wise direction of Gian Lorenzo Bernini, inserting the twin churches of Santa Maria dei Miracoli and Santa Maria di Montesanto at the mouth of the Corso as a «felicitous and auspicious entrance». After the Baroque splendour, the piazza was altered again by Giuseppe Valadier, according to the criteria of the Enlightenment. Games, fares and popular shows took place in the Piazza del Popolo. It was the starting point for the famous Bàrberi race during the carnival and the site of capital punishment. Under the Napoleonic government a plan was implemented for the addition of buildings on a monumental scale influenced by the revolutionary neoclassisicm of Giuseppe Valadier. The Piazza thus assumed its expanded form, with the two lateral semicircles and the buildings near the gateway.

Andrea Sansovino,
Monument of Cardinal
Ascanio Basso della Rovere.

48

Caravaggio, Conversion of Saint Paul and Crucifixion of Saint Peter
Santa Maria del Popolo

On the 24th of September in 1600, Caravaggio gave Monsignor Tiberio Cerasi his pledge to paint two paintings portraying the Conversion of Saint Paul and the Crucifixion of Saint Peter for the chapel he had acquired in Santa Maria del Popolo. The rich patron, who had been charmed by the artist's two paintings in San Luigi dei Francesi, wanted to bring the Lombard master together with another protagonist of the new style of the painting of the beginning of the century - Annibale Carracci, whom he had commissioned to paint the alter-piece of the Assumption of the Virgin. However while the latter work was accepted immediately, Caravaggio had his first version of the Conversion rejected. Perhaps it was too emotive, so that in the second copy the artist followed the text of Saint Paul faithfully and decided to present the scene in an atmosphere infused with a sense of absolute stillness and calm, in which the sacred event seems internalised and only symbolically evoked. The scene is set within the warm atmosphere of the stable and seems dominated by the naturalness and calm of the horse held by the groom. The figure of the horse is counterbalanced by the fore-shortened pose of Paul, with arms outstretched to receive the divine revelation, which is represented by rays of light emanating from the top right-hand corner, the only concession to the supernatural. In the case of the Crucifixion of Saint Peter, once more Caravaggio resolves the question of composition by setting the subject in an atmosphere of motionless suspencion. The economy of the composition is defined by the few diagonal lines which serve to highlight the quiet muscular tension of each of the rogues raising the cross and, on the face of Peter, the intense expression already directed «elsewhere». The clear-cut light contrasts with the dark background and further draws attention to the centre of the composition, which is brought closer. The unifying role of the light is prevalent in both works; it brings out the quiet energy of the volumes, forms and colours, the reds, earth tones and whites of the garments, creating dark shadows which fall on the surrounding ground.

External rioni and rioni to the West of the Tiber

49. **Circus Maximus**

50. **Caracalla Thermae**

51. **Pyramid of Gaius Cestius**

52. **Santa Sabina**

53. **Ponte Rotto and Cloaca Maxima**

54-55. **Santa Cecilia in Trastevere**
Arnolfo di Cambio, Ciborium
Pietro Cavallini, *Universal Judgement*

56. **Santa Maria in Trastevere**
Pietro Cavallini, *Stories of the Virgin*

57. **San Pietro in Montorio and Bramante's Tempietto**

58-60. **Villa Farnesina alla Longara**
Raphael's, *Galatea*
Raphael, *The Loggia of Psyche*

61. **Ponte Sant'Angelo**

62. **Castel Sant'Angelo**

Piazza
di Spagna

Quirinale

Piazza
Navona

Piazza
del Campidoglio

o Gianicolense

Colosseo

Foro Romano

62

61

58-60

56

57

54-55

53

52

49

51

50

Circus Maximus

The first brick-built performance spaces began to appear in Rome from the middle of the first century BC. Previously performances had been held in temporary wooden structures, which were set up in the main public spaces of the city. While the theatre had semi-circular tiers of seats it in and was used for plays, miming and comedies, the amphitheatre, with its elliptical plan, was used for gladiatorial combat and hunts. In the Republican Age, the latter were held in circuses, the large tracks in natural valleys which were used for chariot races: the Circus Flaminius and Campus Martius (223 BC), and the Circus Maximus. Here, legend has it that Romulus had invited the Sabine to watch the games in order to kidnap their women. The Roman people followed the course of their games with passion and so the construction of buildings, organisation of performances on religious holidays or special occasions and handing out of corn («panem et circenses») were often used as a means of propaganda by the ruling class to sway the sympathies of the citizens. The Circus Maximus, the largest in the city, was founded in the time of the

kings, in the Valle Murcia, the natural hollow which separates the Palatine and Aventine hills. Originally, the public had to sit on the grassy slopes around the central space, but the circus was gradually turned into a monument with the addition of brick tiers of seats. 600 metres long and 14 metres wide, it could hold 150.000 spectators in the Augustan Age and 250.000 after it was enlarged by Nero. In the centre of the track was the 'spina', (backbone) a long wall decorated with fountains, statues, altars and obelisks. At either end the chariots had to run round the turning posts, which had three points on the top. A device placed on the spina, with seven stone eggs and seven bronze dolphins, to match the number of laps, recorded the progress of the contest. On one of the short sides there were 12 carceres, the stalls where the runners were held before the start. The circus was rebuilt several times during the Empire and

the last time it was used, was for the games held by Totila in 549 AD.

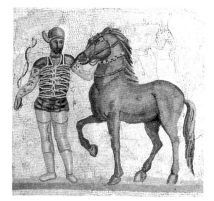

Details of Charioteers in the four factions. Rome, Museo Nazionale Romano. (Palazzo Massimo alle Terme).

Facing page:
The Circus Maximus in a three-dimensional reconstruction of Ancient Rome. Rome, Museo della Civiltà Romana.

Caracalla Thermae

Baths were very common in every part of the Empire in Roman times. Besides the bathing areas and the palaestrae (gyms), they were endowed with gardens, nymphaea, libraries, auditoria, places for shows and games and for keeping food and drinks. These diversions had turned attendance at the baths into the habitual and favourite pastime of the Romans, who spent many hours of the day there, devoting themselves to the care of the body and spirit. The baths became places for social gatherings and centres for the diffusion of culture. During the Imperial Age, the construction of thermal water buildings was an integral part of the political-propaganda programme of the

emperors, who required ever bigger and better organised establishments, a genuine «public service», with free entry for the masses. Caracalla's Baths, which are second only to those of Diocletian, are one of the best preserved thermal complexes of antiquity. Probably planned at the time of Septimus Severus, the baths were inaugurated by Marcus Aurelius Antoninus Basianus, known as Caracalla, in 216 AD, in the XIIth regio or district, (Piscina Publica), situated in the southern part of the city. The area had been filled with monuments by the Severi, including a splendid nymphaeum with several storeys, built on the south-western slopes of the Palatine Hill, and the Via Nova, the road

leading towards the Baths. They were finished in 235AD and were still working in 537AD when, after the siege of Rome by the Goths, the aqueducts were cut off to deprive the city of water.

Pyramid of Gaius Cestius

Originally, the pyramid was outside the city, on the Via Ostiensis, even though it became amalgamated as a defensive buttress in the Mura Aureliane, when they were built in the third century AD. Inscriptions engraved on the sides record that it was built in less than 330 days. It is likely to have been built between 18 and 12BC and has been identified as the funerary monument of Gaius Cestius, an important magistrate, who probably became rich in Asia Minor through trade and tax collection. The impressive tomb is obviously based on Egyptian models, like that of the Quintilus brothers on the Via Appia or the one in the Vatican, known in the Middle Ages as the tomb of Romulus, whereas Cestius' pyramid was identified with the tomb of Remus. The imposing monument, 36 metres high by almost 30 wide, is faced with marble slabs, and was richly adorned with bronze statues of the deceased and four columns at the corners. The rectangular funerary cell was covered with barrel vaulting, faced with tiles and decorated with paintings of the third stile, extolling the virtues of the deceased.

Santa Sabina

The Basilica of Santa Sabina is situated on the slopes of the Aventine. Its foundations, which document almost a thousand years of history, testify to the lively building activity, which, in antiquity, had as its backdrop this hill which was then so rich in springs and vegetation. The Roman aristocratic families had built their sumptuous dwellings here, near the two thermal centres. The crypt of Santa Sabina bears the traces of a Christian community, which was given hospitality in the house of a Roman matron, Sabina, who had been converted to Christianity by her slave Serafia and who was subsequently decapitated during the Empire of Vespasiano. Later, in the Early Middle Ages, the Aventine was selected by monks and the religious as the seat of their hermitages or little fraternal communities. In this context, from the Vth century onwards, one of the most imposing Paleo-Christian basilicas of the city sprang up. The IVth century floor of the former domus is all that remains of it, and it can be viewed through a grating near the entrance to the basilica, but many pieces of walling lie beneath the right aisle. The basilica was built in the Vth century and dedicated to San Domenico in 1222. Some restoration work was carried out in the XVth century, but it was the alterations by Domenico Fontana in 1587, at the time of Sixtus V, and Francesco Borromini in 1643, which would change the interior of the basilical complex fundamentally. Domenico Fontana demolished the schola cantorum, the iconostasis and the ciborium, introducing the main altar and large baldacchino. In the early twentieth century Antonio Muñoz eliminated these changes to restore the church to its original appearance. Three spacious aisles with solemn classical proportions, divided up by twenty-four Corinthian columns, create a majestic internal space based on Ravenna prototypes. This is one of the first basilical exemplars where the columns bear arches rather than trabeations. Originally the church was faced in rich mosaics of which only a fragment remains above the door. There is a metrical inscription in gold lettering alluding to Pietro d'Illiria, who built the church, Celestine I, during whose pontificate it was built, and to the Council of Ephesus. The walls of the church were also faced with marble inlay.

Ponte Rotto and Cloaca Maxima

The bridges prove how skilful the engineers of Rome were, managing to construct robust and impressive structures from foundations thrown into moulds in the water.

Thanks to developments in techniques for making concrete, it was possible to build the first fixed bridge in Rome, the Pons Aemilius. Known today as the Ponte Rotto (Broken Bridge), it is opposite the Foro Boario (cattle fair) and only one of the six original arches remains. Legend attributes the building of the piers to the censors, Marcus Aemilius Lepidus and Marcus Fulvius Nobilior, in 179 BC, with the arches being added by the censors Lucius Mumius and Scipio Aemilius. It is, however, more likely that they probably carried out renovations to a more antique structure, when the Via Aurelia was opened, as the bridge formed the entrance into the city there. The Pons Aemilius underwent periods of damage and restoration from the XIIIth century onwards, and was abandoned after the flood of 1598.

On the opposite side, the outlet of the Cloaca Maxima can be seen, in a large opening carved out of the mud bank. Numerous sources relate that, at the end of the VIIth century BC, Tarquinius Priscus, the first king of the Etruscan dynasty of the Tarquins, initiated a series of public works dedicated to changing the face of the city. In particular, the building of an impressive system of drains (cloacae) was started.

The aim was to drain the marshy areas round the Forum and the hills of the city, and it was finished by the last King of Rome, Tarquin the Proud. The Cloaca Maxima, the largest antique drain known, was used to channel the water from the Velabro, which crossed the valley of the Forum. Partly used as a sewer, it has a diameter of three metres and passes under the Forum of Nerva, the Roman Forum and the Velabro. It discharges into the Tiber near the Ponte Rotto through a stone arch inserted in a wall of tufa in Grotta Oscura, which formed the border of the road before the construction of the modern Lungotevere.

Arnolfo di Cambio, Ciborium
Santa Cecilia in Trastevere

The signature of Arnolfo (Hoc opus fecit Arnolfus) and the date 20 November 1293, are carved on a little pillar of the ciborium of Santa Cecilia. In this case, as in that of San Paolo, members of the workshop must have collaborated on the work. Compared to the ciborium of the Basilica di San Paolo, there is a notable development in the artist's style. In particular it has been remarked that, in this case, more solid links have been forged by the sculptor with classical culture, albeit the re-reading is in a highly personal key.

Compared to the San Paolo ciborium, for example, the treatment by the sculptor of the rapport between forms and space is novel, and of necessity also entails a new figurative conception.

Above all, the proportional relationship between single elements of the framework is different.

The columns have more impetus even though the actual ciborium is, ironically, more compact in height.

More emphasis is given to the figures, which protrude beyond the rectilinear lines of the ciborium.

The single sculptures appear mobile and dynamic within the spaces assigned to them. Subtle, psychological, pictorial, dynamic vibrations and anxieties feature in their stance and expressions.

Pietro Cavallini, Universal Judgement
Santa Cecilia in Trastevere

It was the rediscovery, in 1899, of the surviving frescoes by Cavallini in the convent of Santa Cecilia, which brought up the problem of the identity of the Roman painter. He was celebrated by Ghiberti in his Commentari as the most important of his time, and mention was made of a substantial group of works attributed to him and now mainly lost. The most representative work of Pietro Cavallini is in fact the cycle of frescoes in Santa Cecilia in Trastevere, which were probably executed in the same period as the Arnolfian ciborium, in about 1293. In the Judgement, Cavallini distances himself from, and surpasses, the Byzantine vision.

Either side of the mandorla containing Christ, the figures of the apostles are placed on thrones, which are painted in perspective. The rhythm of the composition is influenced by a dimension of restrained classicism which has none of the crowding and narrative detail of Byzantine painting. Monumentality and solemnity are new elements in Cavallinian painting. The faces of Christ and the apostles seem modelled by a delicate rapport of light and shadow. Compared to the mosaic in Santa Maria in Trastevere, the fresco technique also gives the painter more stylistic freedom in the representation of drapery, which is soft and natural, with greater chiaroscuro.

The work therefore acquires a three-dimensional quality and an expressive power of greater dramatic depth. The expressionistic interpretation of the figures is replaced with a typically Western rationalisation of humanity.

Seraphin, and, above,
Two Saints, details of
Universal Judgement.

Head of Christ, detail
of *Universal Judgement*.

Pietro Cavallini, Stories of the Virgin
Santa Maria in Trastevere

Pietro Cavallini was born in about 1250 and died when he was almost a centenarian, after a long, fortunate and active life, working for prestigious patrons in the major Roman and Neapolitan churches. His oldest surviving work is the mosaic decoration in the apse of Santa Maria in Trastevere. The date and attribution of the body of work, which is referred to by Ghiberti, was confirmed by an inscription, which was present in 1857 and then disappeared. The decoration was commissioned by Bertoldo Di Pietro Stefaneschi, who became parish priest of Santa Maria in Trastevere. The scenes represent the six episodes from the life of the Virgin and a figure of the patron presented to the Virgin by Saint Peter. In each panel the depiction of the episodes is given ample space and light. Order, moderation and clarity are the criteria on which the work is based. The influence of Byzantine models is evident in the iconographic organisation, but often this is more naturalistic in terms of space. Some scholars have drawn attention to the effect Cavallini's contact with the work of Arnolfo di Cambio had on the classical rhythm of his style. However, the individual personality of the Roman painter is

already noticeable in these mosaics. Colour assumes a special role in the original way in which forms are constructed, with a predilection for intense and liberal use of shadows, which make the placid solemnity of the figure stand out, and even in the creation of realistic physiognomies capable of expressing noble holiness and human fulfilment at the same time. The highly poetic and powerfully individual qualities of Cavallinian art constitute a turning point in late medieval painting in the Roman and Neapolitan context and Umbrian XIVth century painting.

Pietro Cavallini, *Birth of Mary.*

Pietro Cavallini, *Annunciation.*

San Pietro in Montorio and Bramante's Tempietto

Built on the top of the Granicolo, the tempietto (little temple) was commissioned by the King of Spain to consecrate the place in which, according to medieval tradition, St Peter, the martyr, founder of the Christian Church and first pope, had been crucified. The young architect Bramante conceived it as a genuine martyrium in antique style, with a central plan and a circle of perimeter columns. The building must have been placed in a large square, which, however, was never built. In spite of the reduced size, the space has been planned in grandiose, monumental style. It is evidently based on the study of the rules of harmony of the Roman Vitruvius, who advised the use of the Doric order of columns for buildings dedicated to masculine divinities or mythological figures famous for their strength and courage. The architect Bramante did in fact use the Doric order for the tempietto, giving it an air of rigour and economy, which is also due to limited use of excessive decoration and the sober harmony of the volumes.

Sebastiano del Piombo,
Flagellation.

Villa Farnesina alla Longara

The Villa Farnesina, one of the jewels of early 16th century Roman classicism, was known as the «Incomparable matchless pearl». It was built in the Trastevere rione between 1506 and 1510, with alterations which lasted until 1520, by Baldassarre Peruzzi, for the Sienese banker, Agostino Chigi. In 1590 it passed to the Farnese, from whom it took its present name. It was the first noble suburban villa in Rome and is a model of balance, harmony and proportion. It has two floors and is in the shape of a horseshoe, which opens onto the garden with a ground floor loggia made up of five arches, which now have protective glass. The loggia was used as a stage for festivities and theatrical performances organised by the owner, which contemporaries recall as being particularly sumptuous. The facade has two tiers, superimposed by Doric pilasters strips, and is crowned by a tall frieze sculpted with festoons of cherubs. Baldassarre Peruzzi was also very much involved with the interior painted and stucco-work decoration. These reveal the same skill in perspective as the wall frescoes, which depict external spaces, making external nature and the interior spaces of the villa seem one. The loggia, in particular, painted with a braid of festoons, was treated as a continuum of the garden. It is decorated with frescoes of the story of Cupid and Psyche, from Apuleius, by Raphael and his pupils. Besides Raphael, Sebastiano del Piombo also worked on the Sala di Galatea, adjoining the loggia, with its Peruzzi ceiling. This is articulated in geometric spaces divided by painted architectural elements which link to the walls. On the floor above is the Salone delle Prospettive (room of views) painted with a trompe l'oeuil loggia; between the pretence architectural features there are Roman trompe l'oeuil landscapes including a vista of Trastevere. Now the villa houses the Accademia dei Lincei and the Gabinetto dei Disegni e delle Stampe, the national graphic collection.

Sebastiano del Piombo,
Polyphemus.

In the suburban villa at the foot of the Gianicolo, known as La Farnesina and built by Agostino Chigi da Baldassarre Peruzzi, Raphael painted a series of frescoes permeated by a profound passion for classic and antique culture. On the ceiling of a loggia which faced directly onto the garden of the villa, Peruzzi had designed a large fresco, which was then painted by Sebastiano del Piombo. The latter had painted the figure of the Cyclops, Polyphemus, on the walls, and beside it, between the end of 1511 and the beginning of 1512, Raphael painted the fresco of The Triumph of Galatea. Taking the subject from a theme based on classical texts, from Ovid's Metamorphosis to Poliziano's Giostra, the painter portrayed the Nereid on a shell drawn by dolphins, surrounded by her train of nymphs and tritons. Three Cupids are unleashing their arrows towards the latter, while the unconscious Galatea, her eyes turned heavenwards, is enraptured by a more elevated form of love, to which the sensuality expressed by the other figures is alien: a platonic love, symbolically represented by the cherub withholding rather than shooting his arrows. Raphael paints the fresco competing with antique painting and statuary, whose language he emulates to perfection; Galatea is portrayed as a Greek Aphrodite, while the chromatic range, like the Pompeiian red, recalls that of Roman paintings.

Raphael, The Loggia of Psyche
Villa Farnesina

As in the Galatea, the frescoes of the Loggia of Psyche reveal the extent to which Raphael was saturated with the culture of antiquity. Raphael was commissioned to paint the new cycle of frescoes in the loggia of Villa Farnesina on the occasion of the wedding on the 28th of August of Agostino Chigi and Francesca Ordeaschi, a Venetian girl whom the banker had brought with him to Rome in 1511. The myth of Cupid and Psyche, recounted in The Golden Ass of Apuleius, was the theme chosen by Raphael; an initiatory story on the troubles of the human soul before the consciousness of love, and being elevated to the dignity of the gods. From the cycle planned by Raphael, the remaining scenes are on the ceiling and pendentives, which are devoted to the heavenly episodes; originally the myth should have continued in the lunettes underneath, with scenes set half way between earth and sky, with the earthly events along the walls. The artist conceived of an ingenious system of architectural trompe l'oeuil: festive garlands of fruits which form a luxuriant pergola as background to the loggia and the garden in front.

Venus, *Ceres and Juno.*   *Cupid and the Graces.*

Ponte Sant'Angelo

Rome was born on the Tiber and thanks to the Tiber. The river offered great advantages as a means of navigable communication and because of the presence of precious salt marshes in the estuary, but due to its irregular flow and frequent floods, it required constant attention, monitoring and maintenance. The construction of the Lungotevere and the large banks after the Unification of Italy changed the road network of the city, which had always converged on the Tiber and the means of crossing it. According to tradition, it was King Ancus Marcius (640-616 BC) who furnished Rome with the first bridge corresponding to the ford downstream from the Isola Tiberina: the Pons Sublicius, whose name refers to the wooden beams (sublicae) with which it is built. Near this, in the second century BC, the first stone bridge, the Pons Aemilius was built. Many of the bridges still used today were built in antiquity, the Ponte Sisto was installed in the XVth century on the remains of the one erected by Agrippa, to join the properties he possessed on both of the river banks, in the Campus Martius and in Trastevere. Another bridge which became very important in terms of its strategic position was the Pons Aelius (134 AD), by which the mausoleum of the Emperor Hadrian could be reached – today's Ponte Sant'Angelo, adorned with the splendid sculptures of the School of Bernini.

Paolo Naldini, *Two Angels*.

Castel Sant'Angelo

The Tiber is dominated by the impressive Mole of Hadrian, built at the behest of the Emperor, probably designed by him and conceived as his personal mausoleum and tomb. Begun in about 123 AD and finished a year after the death of the Emperor by Antoninus Pius, it became the burial place of the Roman emperors up to Caracalla. To reach the mausoleum Hadrian had a bridge specially built opposite the entrance to the majestic building. The mausoleum was in the form of a square at whose corners there were statuary groups. Today the corners of the massive structure are reinforced by bastions erected in the course of the XVIth century on the Pope's wishes, and there are monuments which increase the security and isolation of the mausoleum, which had the appearance of a small fortified village. The tour of the museum inside includes superb cycles of frescoes from the School of Raphael, such as the frieze by Perin del Vaga recounting the tale of Cupid and Psyche, from 1545-1547, and the frescoes of the apartment of Pope Paul III which are attributed to the young Pellegrino Tibaldi.

View towards city and hall of Apollo.

Vatican City

71

72-81

Città
del Vaticano

4-67

63 Piazza
San Pietro

Piazza
Navona

Parco Gianicolense

Saint Peter's square

Emerging from the maze of streets and narrow, unhealthy alleys of the Borgo rione, the visitor of the past left behind them the so-called spina (thorn), which, as can be seen in photographs of the time, closed the opening of St Peter's Square up to the 1930s. Suddenly, in all its splendour, the vast square of Saint Peter appeared in front of them. As part of a project proposed in about 1932 by Marcello Piacentini, but only finished in the Holy Year of 1950, the long stretch of Via della Conciliazione was opened. Although the new solution privileged view from a distance of the facade and dome, on the other hand it diminished the effect of unexpectedness, the grand reception which had enchanted visitors for centuries. This was the final act in the definitive transformation of the area of Saint Peter's Square which had developed gradually in the course of the centuries. In 1586, Sixtus V was the first to endow the space with a theatrical and monumental aspect, when he engaged Domenico Fontana to move the red granite obelisque to the centre of the piazza, whose symbolic focal point it then became. Gian Lorenzo Bernini, commissioned by Alessandro VII Chigi, studied the new layout of the piazza, on which he worked for ten years from 1657 to 1667, turning it into one of the most spectacular architectural achievements of Baroque Rome. Starting with a choice which revealed his classical vocation, Bernini replaced the Corinthian order with Doric columns, placing them in such a way as to form three passages, the middle one having wider barrel vaulting and the side ones narrower, coffered ceilings. There are two hundred and eighty-four columns and eighty travertine piers in all, and a trabeation crowned by a series of one hundred and forty statues of saints and six large coats of arms of Pope Chigi. To avoid

a possible effect of disequilibrium due to the use of the crescent and, at the same time, to orchestrate the piazza from the point of view of perspective, Bernini placed the four rows of columns radially, and gradually increased their diameter, thus ensuring that the proportional relations between the spaces and the columns also remained unchanged in the outside row.

Saint Peter's

It was the Emperor Constantine who instigated the construction of the first basilica, in about the year 320, on the site traditionally thought to be that of the tomb of the apostle Peter. It was finished at the time of the pontiff Liberius (352-366) and its layout has been handed down through iconographic and documentary sources. A building with a basilica's blueprint, it was articulated in five aisles and ended in a transept defined on both sides by exedras. Access was gained through a vast quadriportico atrium, the facade of which gave on to the loggia of the Blessings. On the side of the entrance of the quadriportico was the famous Navicella mosaic by Giotto and his school. Embellished by furnishings, mosaics and monuments in the course of the Middle Ages, it was in the XVth century that the antique basilica attained its greatest splendour, housing important funerary monuments made by the major artists of the time. On the other hand, serious subsidence problems were threatening the fabric of the building at the time when Pope Nicholas decided to rebuild and enlarge the church, but his death in 1455 led to the works being suspended. In the early XVIth century Julius II engaged Donato Bramante to plan the reconstruction of the building, which, apart from housing his own mausoleum, was intended to signal the definitive triumph of a Rome restored to splendour as the ancient imperial city, and capital of Christianity and of the Church State. Bramante conceived the new Saint Peter's as a monumental organism in the form of a Greek cross contained within a square, crowned with a central semi-spherical dome. In form and diameter it was to be similar to that of the Pantheon, and surrounded by four smaller domes inserted between four minor arms, completed by four corner bell towers. After Bramante died suddenly in 1514, Leo X engaged Raphael to continue with the construction, then Antonio da Sangallo and finally, in 1546, Michelangelo. The latter went back to the design of Bramante and conceived of a building in the grand style, but simplified in form, covered by a dome which was intended as the central element of the complex. Modelled almost in the same way as a sculpture, the Michelangelesque dome is vibrant, elastic and imposing. Giacomo Della Porta finished it in 1598, keeping to the general lines of the model left by Michelangelo, without following them with complete fidelity, but rather emphasising the verticalism. With Pope Paul V, the basilica took on its final appearance, until on 18th November 1626, Urban VIII celebrated the consecration of the new temple.

Michelangelo's Pietà
Saint Peter's

In 1498 Cardinal Bilhéres de Lagraulas, Abbot of San Dionigi and Ambassador of Charles VIII, gave Buonarroti the commission for the very famous sculptural group, which was to be placed in the Chapel of Santa Petronilla in the ancient Basilica of Saint Peter. The same patron asked the artist to follow a northern iconographic model of the Virgin holding the body of her son in her arms after the deposition from the cross. As opposed to the composition of the German original, frozen in an unnatural scheme, Michelangelo, however, preferred to create an image of extreme naturalness, with soft, fluid lines. It is the only work signed by him, on the sash which crosses the

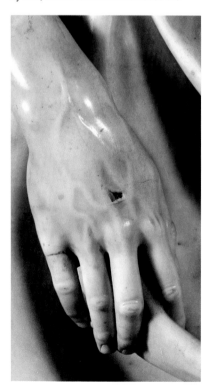

Virgin's breast. The signature, according to Vasari, indicated the pride of the artist in his achievement. The lyrical intensity of the work, the refined smoothness of the marble and the plasticity of the forms all contribute to make it a work of perfect equilibrium. The absorbed expression on the face of Mary reveals her withheld grief; the body of Jesus, surrendered in exhaustion to the immense pain it has borne, brings the holy scene into the dimension of humanity; the fineness of the garments, the monumental composition and the perfection of the features and

anatomy endow the scene with a divine aura and timelessness. Perhaps it was this «absolute» beauty which led to the famous episode so frequently mentioned since, when, on Whit Sunday May 21st 1972, a madman attacked the group with a hammer, entailing a lengthy period of restoration to repair the damage and fill the holes.

Gian Lorenzo Bernini, Baldacchino
Saint Peter's

As soon as he was elected pontiff, Urban VIII, of the powerful Barberini family, chose Gian Lorenzo Bernini, the sculptor and painter, to take charge of the works required to finish Saint Peter's. In particular, he was to be responsible for the «larger structure» which was to tower above the centre of the presbytery, the high altar, under the Michelangelesque dome. The vast size of the architectural feature cum sculpture which Bernini produced is not immediately noticeable, both because of the well-balanced proportions and because of the rich decoration with which the surfaces of the splendid baldacchino are encrusted. It confirmed the artist as the interpreter who had a greater capacity than any other to translate the figurative baroque image of the Church triumphant into form. With imagination, ingeniousness and clever planning, he invented the artifice with unequalled virtuosity, enlisting nature, light and space in his theatrical production. He was constantly searching for dramatic effects, trying to combine all the arts in a single work, in which the light was very skilfully controlled. When it was finished in 1633, the baldacchino, which glorified God the Father as well as the Barberini line, had already made a great impression on his contemporaries thanks to its merits: the richness of the contrasts – the play of bronze-coloured black and gold; the unequalled size – it was over 28 metres high; the dynamism of the forms, which simulate the movement of the canopy; the inextricable fusion of sculpture and architecture in this brilliant transcendence of the borders between the arts.

The Apse Cathedra
Saint Peter's

Although it is equal in size to the arms of the transept, the apse seems larger and more majestic, as it is joined on to the nave and seems like an extension of it. Between the two great background pilaster strips, the Chair of Peter towers over the apse. Between 1656 and 1665, this triumphant vision of bronze and gilt, fruit of the baroque genius of Gian Lorenzo Bernini, was executed under the patronage of Alexander VII Chigi. Within the bronze structure is the ancient wooden chair claimed by legend to be that of Saint Peter. The architecture is vibrant and rather than appearing superimposed on the structure of the building, the artist's design is like a festive decoration. Held up by four imposing figures of saints, the chair seems chiselled and is decorated with golden arabesques. Above it, Bernini exploits the source of light from the central window of the apse, creating a glorious swirling group of angels and cherubs, amongst clouds and dazzling rays, flying round the window featuring the dove of the Holy Spirit. Bernini's work embodies the idea, with all its nuances, of the felicitous union of painting, sculpture and architecture in a single work, in the manner of the poetics of synthesis of Filippo Baldinucci. The imposing papal tombs of Paul III Farnese and Urban VIII Barberini are on either side of the apse in large niches. The funerary monument of Pope Paul III, by Guglielmo della Porta, was the first of the papal tombs to be erected in the new basilica. The Michelangelesque-type structure places the bronze statue of the figure of the Pope at the apex. The monument to Urban VIII was made by Gian Lorenzo Bernini between 1627 and 1647.

It is animated by an intense vitality and enhanced by the soft beauty of the two female allegorical figures symbolising Justice and Charity, apart from the realistically chubby cherubs and the majestic authority of the bronze statue of the Pope. The young Giovan Battista Soria was responsible for the construction of the niche and its marble facing before the monument was placed in it.

Gian Lorenzo Bernini,
*Funerary monument
of Urban VIII.*

Guglielmo della Porta,
Tomb of Paul III.

Giotto, Stefaneschi Polyptych
Vatican Museums, Pinacoteca

Commissioned by Cardinal Jacopo Caetani Stefaneschi, very probably to be placed above the main altar of St Peter's Basilica in Rome, the precious and monumental polyptych is decorated on both sides and divided into three compartments – the central one being slightly larger – with figures contained within Gothic architectural frames. It now has a modern frame and, on the front side, Saint Peter is depicted enthroned in opulent papal garments. There is an enthroned Virgin in the predella in the centre of the back side. Its date is controversial, but in the monumentality of the figures and the compositional complexity, it is stylistically similar to the late works of Giotto. Besides the

polyptych, there are other Roman works by Giotto connected to the name of the same patron: the Navicella mosaic, of which the original is lost, and the fresco decoration of the apse of the basilica, which was destroyed in the XVIIth century alterations to the building. The throne and Cosmatesque floor of the central scene are firmly in perspective. The inventiveness of the polyptych within the polyptych itself is extraordinarily modern. There is a strange mixture of stately, almost archaic and very modern, vivacious characteristics in the panel. The holiness of the images of Peter on one side, and Christ on the other, determined the painter's choice of a strictly symmetrical and frontal depiction. The diffuse, intense light leaves little space for the use of chiaroscuro, and is almost reminiscent of sacred Byzantine art. The way in which the angels are placed in superimposed rows, particularly in the panel of Christ enthroned, recalls the XIIIth century masters. The flat, two-dimensional quality of the decorated cloth behind Christ adds to the archaic effect. On the other hand, the scenes in the side panels are full of movement and vivacity, which is heightened by the refined chromatic choices. This is an extraordinary work from the point of view of colour; the matching is lively and the tones rare and precious. Although the workshop undoubtedly made a significant contribution to the work, Giotto must have been responsible for the overall composition, with its treatment of the rich panel as an architectural feat, almost «a poem».

Filippo Lippi, Incoronation of the Virgin
Vatican Museums, Pinacoteca

The altarpiece of the Incoronation was painted by Filippo Lippi as a commission for Carlo Marsuppini, chancellor of the Republic of Florence, for the Church of the Olivetani Convent in Arezzo, on the occasion of the death of his father, Gregorio, in 1444. The work is divided into three compartments. The Incoronation of the Virgin is in the centre and in the right-hand one the donor appears with two saints and, above the three steps of the podium, there are angels playing music. This scene is repeated in the left-hand compartment. Originally, however, it was a single large panel and probably also had a predella. The painting remained in Arezzo until the Napoleonic dissolution in 1785, when it ended up in private hands, and was then acquired by Pope Gregory XVI. The Virgin is placed in the centre of the scene at the top of some steps on each of which stands a sacred character. At the sides there are angels playing music and, in the foreground, saints and donors. With the exception of Rowlands (1989), the work is attributed to Lippi. The splendid crowd of characters and illusionistic virtuosity of the contemporary Maringhi Incoronation (Florence, Uffizi) are absent in the panel; on the contrary, it is rather restrained, probably a condition of the monastic patronage. In its archaic tone it is similar to the compositions of Angelico. Another hand has been identified in the figures of the music-playing angels, which could be that of the Master of the Nativity of Castello or the Master of the Barberini panels, or Fra Carnevale, referred to as «disciple» of Lippi between the end of 1445 and the beginning of 1446, in the payment accounts.

Raphael, Madonna di Foligno
Vatican Museums, Pinacoteca

The great fame Raphael acquired so quickly in Rome, as a result of his commission to decorate the rooms in the Vatican Palaces, led to his being sought out by many important personages in the ecclesiastical hierarchy, as well as those connected to the papal court and the intellectual ambience, who entrusted him with prestigious commissions. One of them was this painting, which Raphael produced between the end of 1511 and the following year, under the patronage of the historian, Sigismondo de' Conti, who was secretary to Julius II and head of the works in Saint Peter's. The work had formerly been on the main altar of the Roman Church of Santa Maria in Aracoeli, where the patron was buried in February 1512, and it was moved by a niece of Sigismondo to the monastery of Sant'Anna di Foligno where she was a nun (hence the derivation of the name by which the painting is commonly known). The panel was taken to Paris in 1797 and, after being given back to the monastery in Foligno, became part of the Vatican collection. The painting features the Virgin and Child seated on a cloud, together with saints who occupy the foreground and the patron kneeling. Instead of the traditional scheme for the sacred conversations, in which the Madonna is usually presented seated on a throne, Raphael uses a different compositional effect, with the divinity high in the sky. Raphael infuses the whole composition with an intense devotional elation, through the cumulative effect of the individual characters' gestures. His aim was to involve the faithful more directly.

Giorgio Vasari writes that Raphael «wanted to work alone, without anyone else to help him, on the panel in San Pietro a Montorio, the Transfiguration of Christ». The artist was given the commission in about 1516, by Cardinal Giulio de' Medici, the future Pope Clement VII. The latter intended sending it to his episcopal seat in the Cathedral of Narbonne, together with the Resurrection of Lazarus by Sebastiano del Piombo. In a letter sent to Michelangelo on 2nd July 1518, Sebastiano del Piombo relates how, at that point, Raphael had not begun the painting, but it was finished by 6th April 1520, the day the artist died. It is Raphael's last and as soon as it was seen it aroused enormous interest. The Cardinal also realised immediately how fine the work was, when it was found in the painter's studio after his death.

The Transfiguration was then not sent to Narbonne but placed at the head of the artist's coffin as a token of homage and triumph, and as if it was his spiritual legacy. Later, when Cardinal Giulio gained the pontificate, the work was placed in the Roman Church of San Pietro in Montorio, where it stayed until 1797 when it was moved to Paris. In 1815 it was given back and it became part of the Vatican collection. Raphael studied every single head with special attention, even after he had completed the cartoon of the painting. He combines two episodes in the work: the Transfiguration of Christ on Mount Tabor, which fills the top part of the altarpiece, and, in the lower part, the apostles awaiting the resurrection of the Lord and the miracle of the possession by demons. This episode comes immediately after the

Transfiguration in the synoptic Gospels, although there is no exact connection. The originality of the work lies precisely in the tension which is created by the co-existence of the two parts, the top and bottom, the luminous Christ and the more shadowy area of the possessed, with whom the nine apostles who did not go up to Mount Tabor remained.

Augustus of Prima Porta
Vatican Museums, Pio-Clementine Museum

The statue was discovered on the Via Flaminia on the outskirts of Rome, in the villa of Livia, the wife of Augustus, in Prima Porta, by whose name it is known.
The body is based on the model of the Doriforo, the famous sculpture of the Greek bronze-smith Policleto (Vth century BC), with the weight placed on the right leg, the left leg bent, the right arm stretched out in the orator's gesture and the left one which held a lance. The portrait has the hair-style and idealised features which were to become typical of the copies produced after the acquisition of the name of Augustus.

The Emperor is wearing a richly decorated cuirass over a short tunic and a cloak wound round his sides. The reliefs sculpted on the chest are of figures of divinities and personifications, which symbolise the return of harmony and peace in the world. The scene in the middle depicts the return to the Roman legions of the insignia, which had been lost after the defeat of Carrhae (53 BC). Augustus managed to recover them through a skilful diplomatic move, masqueraded in the Imperial propaganda as a military triumph. The Emperor's head, inclined delicately to the right, has the characteristic features of Augustus: the wide forehead, the furrowed brows, the close together deep-set eyes, the long, straight nose, the thin cheeks beneath prominent cheekbones, the small curved mouth and the pointed chin.
In the official image he wanted of himself as neo-emperor, the physiognomy of Augustus has been remodelled in the light of a formal classicistic language, typical of all Augustan artistic production.
The face takes on a solemn, detached air, elevating the Emperor to a sublime plane. On the forehead are the neatly-ordered stylised locks of hair which are to be found in the numerous well-known copies of the type, as well as, in slightly varied form, in the portraits of the heirs, showing that they belonged to the imperial family.

Apoxyomenos
Vatican Museums, Pio-Clementine Museum

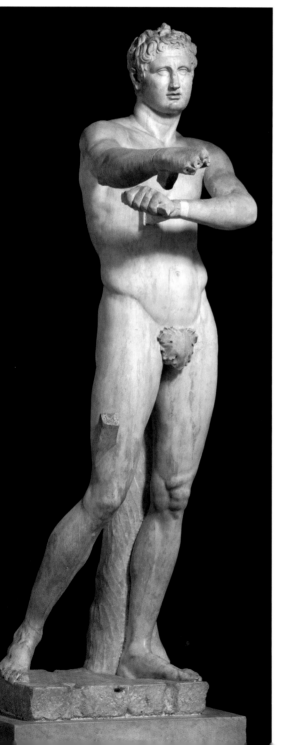

The conquest of Syracuse signalled a turning point in Roman artistic culture. Numerous works of art were brought to Rome at the time; as many arrived after the conquest of Macedonia and, later on, when Corinth was taken. The innumerable works coming to Rome, together with the Greek artists who emigrated to the city, changed its appearance, as well as the taste of the Romans. In due course, a sizeable group of collectors formed and, due to huge demand, works based on classical art and copies of famous Greek originals were produced. The collectors of these works did not concern themselves with distinguishing between copies and originals, and the copies were used as ornamental elements, inserted in architectural complexes. So many copies were produced that there are many more of them compared to the rare original pieces, and, through them, the major Greek artists of the classical age have become known. In particular, the statue of the athlete cleaning himself was found in 1849 in Trastevere, in the ruins of an imperial residence in the area of Vicolo delle Palme, which was later called Vicolo dell'Atleta in honour of the important discovery. The original of the Apoxyomenos is mentioned by Pliny the Elder as one of the works of Lysippus, the bronze sculptor born in Sikyon in about 390 BC. The archetype was cast in about 320 BC and probably brought to Rome from Asia Minor. Pliny recounts that Tiberius, a profound admirer of the Lysippus bronze masterpiece, placed the original in his private home, leaving a copy in its place. The decision provoked a public uprising which obliged the Emperor to restore the Apoxyomenso to the city of Rome. The bronze original was lost, probably in the fire which destroyed Campus Martius in 80AD. The athlete is portrayed in the act of removing the sand and sweat from his body with a strigil, and a copy kept in the Vatican is probably from the Claudian age.

Apollo Belvedere
Vatican Museums, Pio-Clementine Museum

The famous work, which was already known and admired at the end of the XVth century, was moved from the palazzo of Cardinal Giuliano della Rovere, near San Pietro in Vincoli, to the courtyard of the Vatican Belvedere in 1509. The Apollo Belvedere was for a long time considered one of the most beautiful and prestigious sculptures of classical antiquity. In 1764, in his fundamental work, History of Ancient Art, Winckelmann described the admirable sculpture in a very famous passage: « The statue of the Apollo Belvedere is the most sublime of all the antique works which have come down to us. One would say that in this case the artist formed a purely ideal statue, taking from the material only what was absolutely necessary to express and make visible this desire.[...] The sum of its form transcends human nature, and the divine greatness with which it is invested is revealed in the pose». Long considered a Greek original, the statue of Apollo was correctly recognised, during the last century, as a Roman copy from the age of Hadrian, through the bronze models seen by Pausania (I,3,4) in the Agorà in Athens and attributed to Leochares, the Athenian sculptor in about 390 BC.

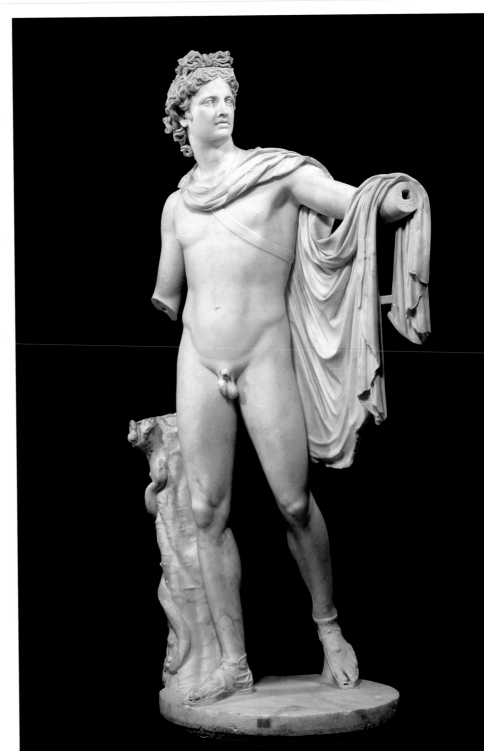

Laocoon
Vatican Museums, Pio-Clementine Museum

The famous sculptural group was found in a vineyard on the Esquiline Hill on 14th January 1506. The work lauded by Pliny the Elder as part of the sculptural furnishing of the Palazzo di Tito was made by the Rhodes sculptors Athanadoros, Hagesandros and Polydoros. The marble was acquired by Pope Julius II in the year of its discovery and placed in the Belvedere Vatican courtyard. The right arm of the central figure, which had been lost at the time of the discovery of the group, which was incorrectly reassembled in the XVIIth century, was recovered by the archaeologist Ludwig Pollak from a Roman stone cutter's workshop in 1905. The work shows Laocoon with his two sons being killed by sea serpents near a shrine, for having cast doubt on the divine nature of the gift of the Trojan horse. The figures are portrayed as already immobilised by the coils of the serpents who have killed the younger son and wounded the father in the left side; the elder son tries in a vain to free himself from the mortal grasp. The discovery of the monumental sculptural groups in the Grotta di Sperlonga, part of the Villa of Tiberius, signed by the same authors as the Laocoon, has fuelled the debate about the work's origin as a Hellenistic original or a copy made at the time of Tiberius from a bronze model of the second half of the second century BC.

Raphael, Vatican Rooms
Vatican Museums

Raphael's great opportunity came in 1508. At the time, Giuliano Della Rovere, Pope Julius II, decided to move to the upper floor of the Vatican Palaces, where there were four new rooms to renovate in the northern area. The work was entrusted to Bramante and began in the Stanza della Segnatura (Room of the Signature) and the Pontiff engaged some of the most well-known artists of the time, among whom was the young Raphael. The artist's success was immediate: the Pope decreed that «all the other masters both old and young should be thrown to the winds» and entrusted the entire decoration to the young man from Urbino. In the Stanza della Segnatura, the space dedicated to the pontiff's library, Raphael departed from the most well known iconographic precedents for his scheme, painting a

sequence of ideal portraits of figures as symbols of knowledge and making them part of a choral action. This was a visual manifestation of the organising concept which informed the union between antique knowledge and Christian revelation. The arrangement of the crowds, the final balance of forces and the space assigned to every detail convey the idea of a spiritual order, which is inherent in all the frescoes in the Stanze. A great airiness, the harmonious juxtaposition of subtle chromatic ranges and accurately studied gestures are salient features of the compositions. In the complex iconographic programme of the rooms, both the spiritual and temporal power of the Church had to be affirmed, with emphasis on the ideal continuity between the greatness of antique Rome and modern, Christian

Rome. In all the frescoes of the first two rooms, the artist demonstrates his capacity to respond to the pontiff's demands with new iconographic solutions, but Julius II died in Rome in February 1513. Raphael then received the commission for the third room, which takes its name from the episode depicted in the only fresco by him for it: the Fire in the Borgo (circa 1514). Critics of the artist have noted the beginning of a new pictorial style in this work, characterised by a heroic sense of classicism and by new preoccupations, which signals the arrival of Mannerism.

Liberation of Saint Peter, Stanza di Eliodoro and detail.

Fire in the Borgo, Stanza dell'Incendio di Borgo.

Raphael, School of Athens
Vatican Museums, Room of the Signature

In the School of Athens (1509), Raphael affirms the centrality of the rational search for the truth, besides receptiveness towards the wisdom of the ancients, which is celebrated here, in the context of the decorative project for the rooms of a Catholic Pope in the Renaissance Age. The philosophers and sages of antiquity are placed within the splendid classical architecture. In the centre are the figures of Plato and Aristotle, indicating the sky and the earth respectively. The measured and eloquent gestures signify philosophy, and the faces of Raphael's contemporaries are used for the sages of the past: Michelangelo, who was painting the ceiling of the Sistine Chapel at the same time, is recognisable in the figure of Heraclitus, seated and leaning with his left elbow on the first step of the staircase. The perspective creates a very effective framework for the scene, enabling an immediate reading of the message and role of the characters represented. This is aided by the light which floods the scene, infusing it with solemnity and clarity. In short, this scenario in the grand style celebrates the continuity between the antique and the modern, the great philosophy of the pagan age and the greatness of the Church.

15th-Century Frescoes in the Sistine Chapel
Vatican Museums

The explicit purpose of the iconographic programme of the Sistine Chapel, which was built in the Vatican Palaces complex between 1477 and 1481, to the design of the architect Baccio Pontelli, was to underline the pontifical authority of Sixtus IV della Rovere who was invested in 1471. The team of Florentine artists engaged by the Pope for the enterprise is thought by modern critics to have been led by Perugino, who only began to work in 1480 on establishing the general criteria for the work, the architectural divisions and the dimensions of the figures. From the summer of 1481, Cosimo Rosselli, Botticelli and Ghirlandaio were also engaged. Luca Signorelli and Bartolomeo della Gatta were taken on at the end, and executed, respectively, the Last Days of Moses and the lost Dispute between St Michael and the Devil, works of an extraordinary plastic and inventive power and which exercised no little influence over Michelangelo for the ceiling. Perugino was entrusted with the most important fresco from the doctrinal point of view, the Donation of the Keys, and it is not by chance that his portrait appears beside that of the two architects. The only signature to appear in the whole cycle is also that of the Umbrian master, in the Baptism of Christ. In the middle section on the right are the Stories of Christ and on the left, those of Moses, so that they are opposite one another. The inscriptions above each scene have an explanatory function and are intended to underline the way in which the Moses story prefigures that of Christ. The focal point of the whole cycle is in fact the Donation of the Keys, which reveals how Perugino has assimilated the geometric-mathematical concept of Piero della Francesca. The episode is constructed around a central axis whose visual counterpoint is the top of the tympanum of the Temple of Solomon, depicted in the background, while the shiny expanse of the marble inlay in the square is designed with the geometric device of vanishing points. The scene is very

Sandro Botticelli,
Temptation of Christ.

evocative and is arranged by Perugino in perfect symmetry: the two triumphal arches stand out on the line of the horizon; in the piazza, two groups of little figures seem to portray some other episodes from the Gospels, while in the foreground there are two groups of onlookers who act as wings to the central scene. Set beside the measured compositional order of Perugino is the restless imagination of Botticelli, author of the scene of the Punishment of Korah, Dathan and Abiram. The allusion to those who rebel against Moses is intended to drive home the legitimacy of the supremacy of the Roman Church and the papacy.

Sandro Botticelli,
*Punishment of Korah,
Dathan and Abiram,*
detail.

Perugino,
Donation of the Keys.

Michelangelo, the frescoed ceiling of the Sistine Chapel
Vatican Museums

In 1504, the chapel begun by Sixtus IV in 1477 had revealed serious movement problems, which necessitated consolidation works. Iron chains were inserted into the ceiling with its painted, starry sky and the filling of holes resulted in damage to the former decoration. For this reason Julius II decided to have new frescoes executed by Michelangelo. The iconographic programme was to include the depiction of stories from Genesis, the Prophets and the Ancestors of Christ, and other allegorical figures. In this way the ceiling became the ideal preface to the XVth century narrative cycle on the walls, with the stories of Moses, Jesus and the pontiffs. The work began in 1508 and was carried out almost exclusively by Michelangelo until 1512. The monumental figures are depicted within an architectural cornice in the grand style. This unifies the separate parts, conceived as a succession of triumphal arches, which mark out the route of the pontifical procession from the entrance to the altar. The narrative begins with the vigorous figures of the Prophets and the Sibyls, portrayed on the side walls in larger dimensions than the others, muscular and powerful, in various attitudes, some in absorbed meditation and others caught up in vibrant dynamism. In the central section of the ceiling, Michelangelo depicts nine stories taken from the Book of Genesis. The artist wanted the scenes to be read in reverse order, from those of the creation to the stories of Noah, from whom the Jewish race is descended. However the focal point of the narrative is the Creation of Adam; it is known worldwide and is an emblem of the perfect classicism which informs

Renaissance culture. The whole composition is constructed on transversal lines which run parallel or intercept each other, making the two bodies seem drawn to one another. The tale of Genesis then continues, with the depiction of the stock originating from the three sons of Noah; these are the Ancestors of Christ depicted in the vaulting cells and the lunettes. In the latter in particular, Michelangelo experiments with some of the more innovative solutions of the Sistine cycle. The characters portrayed have a great variety of temperaments; some seemed to ignore the observer, absorbed in private contemplation. The colours are more varied, while the artist's technique is freer and more spontaneous.

Michelangelo, Universal Judgement
Vatican Museums, Sistine Chapel

In 1533, Clement VII was the first person to suggest to Michelangelo that he should paint the Judgement on the walls of the Sistine Chapel. When the Medici pontiff died, the plan was taken up by his successor, Paul III Farnese. The artist began to put up the scaffolding in June 1535. He covered the walls with a layer of bricks, which were thicker at the top than the bottom, so as to produce an inclined surface which would make the work easier to read and avoid dust deposits. A single large compositional structure contains the Judgement, although there is no architectural framework whatsoever: the various parts, from top to bottom, are connected and refer to each other. The sky, painted with lapislazuli, a material as incorruptible and precious as gold, brings unity to the different parts of the scene and has a symbolic function, transporting the vision outside time. Angels with the symbols of the passion are depicted in the top of the lunettes. In the centre, Christ in Judgement and Mary are surrounded by the ranks of the blessed and the saints. In the middle section, angels sound the trumpets of Judgement, while at the sides the just rise upwards and the damned are driven down to the infernal Gods. The last scenes, in the lowest section, portray the resurrection of the bodies and the damned being led to Hell. In 1564, after the Council of Trent, Daniele da Volterra was engaged to add the famous «breeches», to cover what appeared at the time as the excessive nudity of the Judgement. In the recent restoration (1990-1994) some of Volterra's alterations – those applied dry – were eliminated, and, after lengthy cleaning, the fresco has recovered its luminosity and clarity of colours and forms in such a way as to regain both definition in the details and an overall unity of the work. This extraordinary Dantesque vision, this manifestation of the horror of merciless divine judgement, is a clear reference to the church's need to reflect on the destructive events of the Sack of Rome, but it speaks a universal language which propels it well beyond its time, making it capable of reflecting the melancholy and fear, anguish and hope, eroticism and pain, individual and collective tragedy, of contemporary humanity.

IONAS

Beato Angelico, frescoes in the Cappella Niccolina
Vatican Museums

In 1447, a few months after gaining the papal seat, Nicholas V called the Florentine painter to Rome, to decorate a small area of the Vatican Palaces for use as a private chapel for the pontiff. This is how, together with the aid of collaborators, Beato Angelico came to paint the frescoes of the Stories of Saint Stephen and Saint Lawrence, heroes of early Christianity and witnesses of the transition from the still pagan world to the beginning of Christianity. The setting for the scenes is an ideal city, with Renaissance buildings beside those of antiquity. The figures wear modern clothes and there are allusions to living personages; for example, Pope Sixtus II has the face of Nicholas V himself. A noble, almost monumental tone pervades the frescoes of Angelico, from the sculptural definition of the characters to the almost grandiose and cultured architecture with its, in some cases, daring foreshortening. The perfect architectural framework and the solidity of the bodies are the perfect expression of the concept of Christian Humanism, which the pontiff himself advocated. The aim was to reconcile the antique and Christian cultures and to legitimise papal Rome as the heir of Imperial Rome. Beato Angelico's interest in architecture and perspective is also revealed in the scene where Saint Lawrence receives the Treasures of the Church, in which a colonnade hides the Pope from the two armed men entering by a classical doorway, which bears a relief of the Eternal Father on the tympanum. The tale unfolds with an oratorical, and, in some cases, almost fairy-tale-like tone, while the setting appears to reflect the principles of richness, variety and colour, which, in the words of Alberti, give a building «a light and pleasing air». The moderation and order of Florentine Renaissance art are blended with the humanistic culture rich in archeological and architectural passions promoted by Nicholas V himself.

Overleaf:
Saint Lawrence distributing alms.

Top: *Saint Lawrence invested as deacon.*
Left: *Saint Sixtus entrusts Lawrence with the treasures of the church.*

Outside the Walls

95-96 ↑ **92-94** ↑ **85-91** ↑

Villa Borghese

82-84

Piazza di Spagna

Quirinale

Piazza del Campidoglio

Colosseo

Foro Romano

→ **98**

↓ **99**

↓ **100**

Villa Borghese

When in 1605 the pontiff Paul V Borghese was elected, his nephew Cardinal Scipione Borghese became the true father of Rome. Scipione did not exercise this acquired power in affairs of state or political power, to which the so-called Cardinal nephews were normally attracted, but in the satisfaction of his unbridled pleasure in the possession of works of art. To satisfy this desire, he sacrificed every ambition, be it in government or in the family. Scipione Borghese decided to retire from public life when he was only 53, in 1629, when his lifelong friend, Maffeo Barberini (Urban VIII), through whom he would have been able to obtain new power and even political influence, became Pope. From the beginning of the XVIIth century, when he had had his summer house of delights built in the garden outside Porta Pinciana, his foremost intention had in fact been to indulge his very personal vice, the pleasure of collecting beautiful things, masterpieces, antiquities, paintings and sculptures of the XVIth century, by the most well known contemporary artists. Each of these works had to be displayed in its own carefully designed space within a purpose-built architectural context. Guido Reni, Gian Lorenzo Bernini and Caravaggio were some of the Masters who worked for this cardinal of sanguine character, who was overbearing at the same time as being cultured and generous. He was passionate about scientific studies and also cultivated an interest in music, which he indulged in his villa where he possessed various instruments. The Museo Borghese and the Galleria Borghese, which is still known as the «queen of private collections» are still

in the palazzo today. In 1901, after a long legal wrangle, the villa was acquired by the state, and in1903, the park, which was given to the Commune of Rome, was opened to the public. Visiting the Villa Borghese, is, in a way, like taking a journey through the city's cultural and figurative history.

View from the atrium.

Johann Wilhelm Baur,
Villa Borghese.

Borghese Summer House
Villa Borghese

Cardinal Scipione conceived of the summer house as a treasure trove of works of art: here a late XVIth century sobriety in the antique style blends with the precious neo-classical decoration of the late XVIIIth century patrician interiors by Marcantonio IV Borghese. The typology of the Pincian summer house is like that of the suburban XVIth century villa, points of reference being the Farnesina Chigi and the Villa Medici. Two characteristic elements are the little lateral towers, which make it possible to distinguish the villa from the surrounding greenery from a distance, as in the case of the relatively close Villa Medici. Then there is the portico in which antique sculptures are inserted,

and the large, light entrance hall. There are numerous architectural precedents, amongst which, again, the Villa Medici. This solution enabled the immediate display, externally, of the richness of the antique collection, and also animated the facade with a subtle play of full and empty space, and chiaroscuro. During the last restoration, the double flights of steps giving access to the portico was reinstated. After subsidence, in 1795, it had been replaced by a pyramid-shaped staircase. Flaminio Ponzio's original plan had clearly been copied from the Michelangelesque one for the Palazzo Senatorio in Campidoglio, and gave direct access to the open ungated portico. The

numerous windows, and the arcades of the two loggias, a ground floor one at the front and the first floor western one, which were later decorated by Lanfranco with the Council of the Gods, seem to reflect the fundamental nature-architecture rapport which is typical of Palladian Villas. The light is an essential element in summer house architecture and it is maximised by the use of the marble white colour in the external plasterwork, which was only restored in 1995-1997.

Park and Secret Gardens
Villa Borghese

A park covering 80 hectares in the heart of the city, including the part which joins the Mure Aureliane, Porta Pinciana, Piazzale Flaminio and the new districts of Salario and Pinciano, which emerged after the Unification of Italy: this is the Villa Borghese. It is one of the favourite places of Romans and foreigners alike, celebrated in the guide books of every age, described in literature and chosen as a background for countless films. Then there are fields, avenues, little woods and pine forests, gardens and valleys, in a varied landscape full of unexpected vistas, which are themselves an integral part of the architecture of the place. Open spaces punctuated by fountains, monumental elements, statues, sculptural groups, antique remains and statues, woods and hunting areas – the formal, ordered spaces alternated in perfect harmony with the natural, wild landscape. The secret garden in particular is a characteristic of Renaissance and Baroque villas and its origin is the medieval hortus conclusus. Directly connected to the main building, it was protected by walls and contained rare plants. In the Villa of Cardinal Scipione there were two private gardens situated at the sides of the noble summer house: the first was called the «melangoli» (bitter orange) garden and the second, «fiori» (flower) garden. A third was made in about 1680, between the Uccelliera and Meridiana pavilions. Rare and exotic flowers, especially bulbs, were cultivated in it. The two gardens adjoining the side walls of the summer house are a hundred metres long and twenty wide and are surrounded by high and richly decorated walls. The Uccelliera pavilion also belongs to the Scipione period. This is a particularly charming structure, characteristic of the XVIth century villas of the nobility and whose use dates back to Roman times. The Uccelleria was built between 1617 and 1618 under the direction of Giovanni Vasanzio. Both of the Uccelliera facades are crammed with sophisticated travertine and stucco decoration, with large grotesque masks, garlands of flowers, vases and cornucopias overflowing with flowers of every kind, in an explicit dialogue with the garden and flowers around it.

Sleeping Hermaphrodite
Galleria Borghese

The formation of the collection of antique sculptures and paintings which embellished Villa Borghese is owed to the activity of Cardinal Scipione Borghese (1567-1633), nephew of Pope Paul V, at the beginning of the XVIIth century. In 1807, Napoleon forced Camillo Borghese, the husband of his sister Pauline, to sell him most of the archaeological pieces. In the same period the family tried to restore the original collection to its former size through new acquisitions and excavation projects. This is the context in which the statue of the Sleeping Hermaphrodite, a second century AD copy of a Hellenistic original, was added to the villa's decoration in order to replace the similar exemplar restored by Bernini, which had ended up in the Louvre. The imaginative charm of the sculpture lies in the feminine or masculine aspect taken on, according to the spectator's point of view, by the ambiguous son of Hermes and Aphrodite, lying languidly on the mattress (which was restored in the XVIIIth century by Andrea Bergondi).

86

Titian, Sacred and Profane Love
Galleria Borghese

The work was painted by Titian in 1514, when he was 25 years old, for the wedding between Nicolò Aurelio, the Venetian Secretary of the Council of Ten, whose coat of arms is represented on the sarcophagus and Laura Bagarotto, daughter of the judge, from Padova. A fountain decorated with bas relief like an antique sarcophagus fills the long side of the canvas, dividing the painting into two parts. Another caesura is caused by the branches behind the cherub who is stirring the water with his arm. The background is also unusual; on one side there is a church and a flock of sheep, and on the other a fortified city and two rabbits, symbols of love and fertility. Critics have long discussed the marked contrast between the two female figures seated on the edge of the fountain, a contrast which had an illustrious precedent. In fact Pliny recounts that the Greek sculptor Praxiteles had made two sublime statues of Venus, one clothed and one without clothes. The two equally perfect women symbolise on the one hand «brief earthly happiness», with the attribute of the pot of jewels, and the other «eternal heavenly happiness», holding the burning flame of God's love in her hand. The dressed Venus should therefore probably be interpreted as the pure bride who, close to Love, is assisted by the goddess Aphrodite in person. The gesture of the cherub stirring the water, source of life, in a sarcophagus, therefore probably represents love as intermediary between heaven and earth. The title is the result of a late XVIIIth century interpretation based on a moralistic reading of the clothed figure. The universal fame of Titian's work was confirmed in 1899, when Rothschilds the bankers offered a greater price for this painting than the estimated worth of the whole of Villa Borghese including the works of art.

87

Gian Lorenzo Bernini, Apollo and Daphne
Galleria Borghese

In this case, the theme of metamorphosis provides the inspiration for a scene in which the vitality, movement and elegance particular to the baroque aesthetic exist side by side, finding their maximum expression. Bernini focuses his attention on the instant in which the nymph Daphne is transformed into a bay tree, the same instant in which the god Apollo succeeds in catching her up and seizing her. The impetus will be frozen in the most absolute immobility in a few seconds, but Bernini manages to make us feel the last palpitating instant of life in all its painful intensity, the extreme sensation of vitality of that fleeting moment which is inherent in the very dynamics of existence. The commission of the group is dated at the beginning of 1622, when the Rape of

Proserpine was finished, and also came from Scipione Borghese. The prototypes for the figure of Daphne are to be found in the Maenads, in the bas-reliefs on antique sarcophagi. Bernini's profound knowledge of the antique is also evident in the figure of Apollo, based on the Apollo Belvedere in the Vatican Museums, from which, showing a precise philological knowledge of the antique, he even copies the footwear. In this case as well, the artist's aim is to represent several time sequences in a single image. With perfect stage direction he plans the placing of the group in exactly the right place in relation to the observer: on entering the room from the left we first notice Apollo's glance and the unexpected movement towards the nymph, then, standing in front, we become aware

of the details of the metamorphosis, which the artist renders with matchless virtuosity. In the dragon-shaped scroll on the base of the sculpture there is a moralistic inscription, a quotation taken from the Twelve Couplets for a Gallery, written between 1618 and 1620 by Maffeo Barberini, who became Pope Urban VIII: Quisquis amans sequitur fugitave gaudia forme/ fronde manus implet baccas seu carpit amaras» («Whoever in loving pursues the joys of fleeting forms, when reaching for fruit among the branches will pluck only bitterness»).

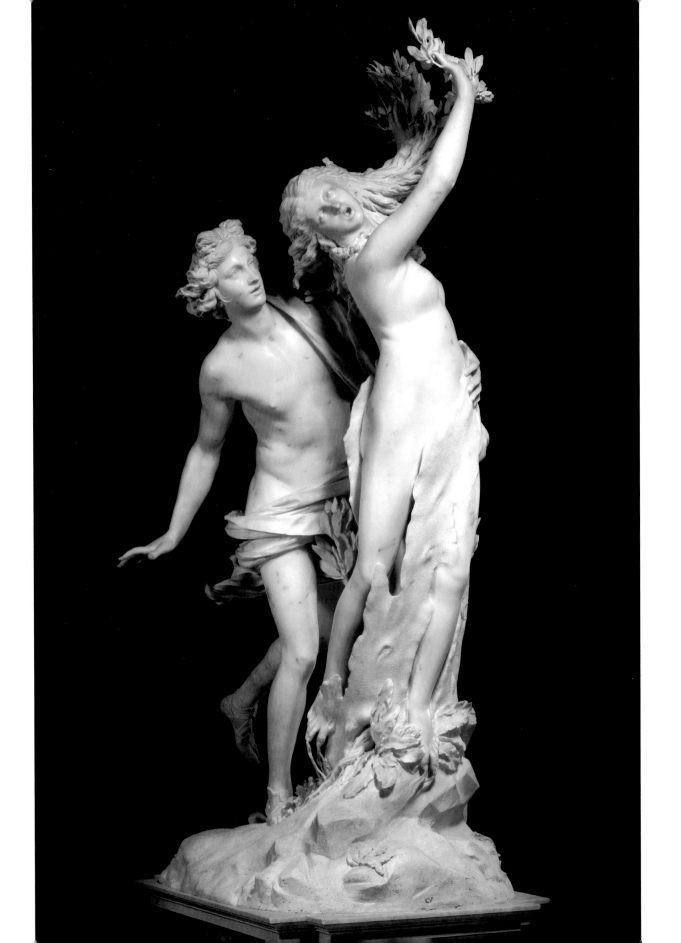

Gian Lorenzo Bernini, The Rape of Proserpine
Galleria Borghese

The work represents the King of the Underworld, Pluto, as he seizes the young Proserpine, daughter of Jove and Ceres, to make her become his wife. Proserpine thus became Queen of the Underworld, while her mother, goddess of the harvest, retreated into solitude, provoking famine and drought. Jove then ordered Pluto to give back the maiden. In the end

Proserpine was allowed to spend two-thirds of the year on the earth and one third with Pluto in the kingdom of the dead. Every time she came back to the kingdom of the living, the earth would also be reborn and covered with flowers. The myth portrayed in the sculpture, taken from Ovid's Metamorphoses and linked to the spring, could also have been an allusion to

the rebirth of the Borghese house after the death of Paul V in 1620. In fact Scipione commissioned Bernini to sculpt the group after Aeneas and Anchises and it was paid for in 1621. From the mythological tale, the sculptor chooses the moment of greatest dynamic tension for his scene, that of the actual rape. The result is a monumental group of remarkable complexity, with the two figures wrapped round each other creating a spiral form, in what is almost an embodiment of the force which produces torsion. Once again, the reference to Hellenistic culture is obvious; the work is a triumph of naturalism and virtuosity. The intertwined forms are thrown vertically into space, unleashed and launched into the air and the light, inciting wonder in the observer. Every detail of the work is aimed at heightening the drama and the whirling dynamism of the composition; even the maiden's hair spreads out in the surrounding space, as if caught by an implacable wind. The wish to represent successive moments of the story synthesised in a single image is new and typically baroque. Seen from the left, the focus is on the power and speed of the stride and the moment in which the «prey» is caught; seen from the front, the conqueror is stilled in triumph; seen from the right the maiden's tears and her prayer to heaven are discernible. The rough strength of the god contrasts with the softness of Proserpine's skin, which is conveyed with that wonderful detail of Pluto's fingers sinking into the young woman's flesh.

Antonio Canova, Pauline Borghese
Galleria Borghese

The Napoleonic age marked the climax of
Canova's international fame; the busts
and statue portraits of members of
Napoleon's family, including the famous
portrait of Pauline Borghese Bonaparte as
Venere Victrix belong to this period.
In her left hand, Napoleon's sister holds
the golden apple by which her beauty had
been recognised by Paris to be superior
to that of two other goddesses,

Juno and Minerva.
The device of placing portrait heads on the
idealised bodies of divinities or heroes was
commonplace in Imperial Roman art,
but the nude portrait of a person of rank
was highly unusual at that time.
Canova was effecting a metamorphosis of
a historical person into an antique divinity.
The work aroused great admiration among
contemporaries; its subtle sensuality

perfectly embodied the ideal of grace in
the theory of Winckelmann «pleasure
through reason».
This is another reason why the marble
portrait of Pauline, with its extremely
smooth forms, was considered the
apex of the neo-classical style.
Antonio Canova had begun to prepare the
work in 1804. We know that when it was
exhibited in the artist's studio in 1808,

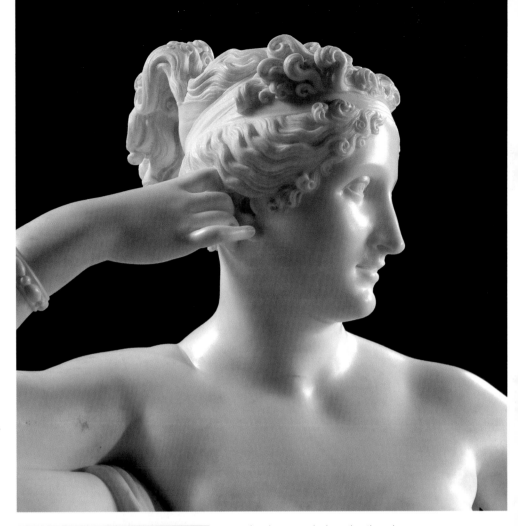

the same year in which Camillo Borghese, the patron of the work and Pauline's husband, completed the payment, it was much visited and admired.
The Borghese prince took the work to Turin and it stayed there until, after the separation from Pauline and the fall of Napoleon, Camillo brought it back to Rome and displayed it in the family palazzo, where the sculpture was also on display at night, lit up by torches.
In this work, the exquisite softness of the modelling and the rapport with antique sarcophagi and Titian's Venus blend to form a perfect balance of «ideal beauty» and «natural beauty».
The marble is supported on the wooden structure of the bed. This conceals a mechanism, used at the time and recently restored, which enables the statue to be

turned on its own axis, inverting the role between the work and the spectator: it is the sculpture which moves, while the observer is impressed by the fleeting images of perfect beauty.

Caravaggio, David with the Head of Goliath
Galleria Borghese

A three-quarters view of David is presented, emerging from behind a dark curtain, sword in hand and proudly intent on observing the head of Goliath, still bleeding after the decapitation. Although the head of the giant is already severed, it is still strongly expressive. The emotive sensitivity expressed on the wrinkled forehead, in the mouth opened in the final breath, and in the intense, suffering glance of Goliath, is also felt in the flesh of the torso and the expression on the face of David. The brown trousers and torn shirt which he is wearing contain passages of great pictorial synthesis, involving the use of long, separate brushstrokes and the juxtaposition, in the case of the shirt, of pure whites and greys, in a subtle play of transparency. Caravaggio used his own self-portrait for the head of Goliath, while in the David the features of his «little Caravaggio» are reproduced. A recent hypothesis suggests that the David is a youthful portrait of the artist, which would make the painting a double self-portrait. With conflicting feelings of disgust and pity, with one hand David brandishes his sword, on whose blade are letters which are not easy to decipher, but which may form the motto «Humilitas Occidit Superbiam»; the biblical hero is in fact a model of virtue. If one accepts the hypothesis that Scipione Borghese had commissioned Caravaggio for the work, it probably belongs to the last Roman period and would therefore be from before 1606. However, some scholars attribute the simplification of forms, the essential quality of the composition and the rapid application of brushstrokes to a later period. In this case the painting may be interpreted as a gift, sent by the artist to Cardinal Scipione Borghese in the expectation of being granted grace, as the last attempt at drawing attention to the desperation of his circumstances and his wish to return to Rome.

91

Giovanni Girolamo Savoldo, Tobias and the Angel
Galleria Borghese

The work portrays the biblical passage in which the angel tells the young Tobias to catch fish in the River Tigris, to cure his father's blindness with gall. Setting the figures frontally side by side, the artist has used the same colours for their garments, red, and a different shade of pure white from that of the wings, which stand out, back lit, against the background vegetation. The head of Tobias is probably taken from the angel in the top panel of Titian's Averoldi polyptych, which came to Brescia in 1522 and made a strong impression on local painters. In fact, when the painting entered the Borghese collection, it was attributed to the great Venetian master. Even though Titianesque painting may have influenced the career of the Brescian artist, critics have not agreed on the work's date. In Savoldo's art, the colouring of Venetian painting blends with the naturalism inherent in Lombard culture; reflections of light in the silver tone of the angel's cloak create metallic, almost lunar flashes. Salvado's considerable research into the use of natural effects in the human figure is evident in the drapery, but also in the branches, which appear ruffled by the air. It was not by chance that the painting of the Lombard master became an essential point of reference for the young Caravaggio, especially in half length portraits of youths with their refined colour and the accentuated chiaroscuro of the backgrounds.

92

Museo Etrusco of Villa Giulia

From a brief period in the VIIth century to the advent of the Republic, in 509BC, Rome gravitated into the Etruscans' sphere of interest. Antique sources relate that Tarquinius Priscus was a rich citizen of Tarquinia who boasted about his descent from a noble and Greek family of Corinth. He had arrived in Rome in search of glory and was elected King by the people. Tarquinius and his successors instigated reforms and implemented substantial urban changes, making Rome a city state on the model of the Greek ones, the largest in central Italy. The Etruscans have come back to Rome thanks to important museum collections founded in the 19th century, like the Museo Nazionale Etrusco of Villa Giulia, which houses some of the most important Etruscan exhibits from Lazio museum collections. The museum was founded in 1889 to accommodate antiquities from the pre-Roman period in Lazio, southern Etruria and Umbria, in its branch at Villa Giulia. The Villa is in the Mannerist style and was built at the behest of Pope Julius II in the Vigna Vecchia area in 1551-1555. From the start, Michelangelo, then Vasari and Vignola, collaborated on the construction, while the decoration is owed to a team of painters, of whom the most prominent were the Zuccari brothers and Giovanni da Udine. The Museum houses material from civilisations flourishing between the Iron Age and the Roman era in Lazio, especially in the north-east area of the region, including that between the Tiber and Tuscany. It was founded in 1889 as a section of the Museo Nazionale Romano for the extra-urban antiquities of the province of Rome, and was later

enlarged with the addition of the famous Castellani and Barberini collections.

Olpe Chigi da Veio, second half of VIIth century BC.

Head of *Hermes* from the sanctuary of Portonaccio a Veio, end of VIth century BC.

Sarcophagus of a Married Couple
Museo Etrusco di Villa Giulia

The terracotta sarcophagus, which was originally painted all over, comes from the necropolis of Banditaccia in Cerveteri and represents one of the masterpieces of clay sculpture from the end of the VIth century BC (circa 520BC). It is actually a large urn for the ashes of the deceased, portraying a married couple reclining on the cushions of the banqueting bed (the kline), with its decorated feet and high mattress. The man, with his broad naked chest, tenderly embraces the shoulders of his elegantly dressed wife. In their hands, the couple must have held objects or foods for the banquet, one of the principal social events for the aristocratic classes, in which, in the Etruscan world, women could participate.

The influence of ionic style is evident in the broad soft surfaces of the bodies, the lower parts of which are less defined, wrapped in the folds of the garment, in the focus on decorative details, and in the style of the elongated faces with convex foreheads, the almond-shaped eyes, the thin noses, protruding chins and typical archaic smiles. Worth noting is the attempt at rendering drapery between the two cushions.

Apollo of Veio
Museo Etrusco di Villa Giulia

The large terracotta statue, which even today still bears a considerable number of traces of the antique paint, was part of the decoration of the Portonaccio temple built in Veio at the end of the VIth century BC (circa 510-500 BC). Together with other statues, it was placed 12 metres up on the beam of the roof ridge. Recent restoration (2004) has restored the colours to their former splendour. The sculpture must have come from the workshop in Vulca, the most important source of terracotta or production in Veio, to which, according to Pliny the Elder, Tarquinius Priscus gave the commission for the cult statue of the Giove Capitolino temple in Rome, which was finished after the advent of the Republic (509 BC). Apollo is portrayed while walking, possibly with a bow in his right hand, in the act of contesting the right of Heracles to the sacred deer of Delphi, as the Greek myth relates. The influence of ionic art is visible in the face lit up by the characteristic archaic smile, the decorative style of the hair with long plaits and the folds of the cloak, which clings to the body, revealing its powerful structure with defined muscles and tendons.

Giacomo Balla, Deer Park
Galleria Nazionale di Arte Moderna

« Giacomo Balla became our 'master' and introduced us to the modern technique of Divisionism without exactly teaching us the basic scientific rules. Balla was a man of absolute integrity; he was profound and thoughtful, and a painter in the broadest sense of the word [...] We were very lucky to meet a man like him, whose decision probably determined the course of our career. The atmosphere in Italian painting was, at the time, as confused and deleterious as you can imagine; in a similar atmosphere even Raphael would only have got as far as genre painting!» wrote Gino Severini in 1946, highlighting a fundamental role played by Giacomo Balla in the views of Villa Borghese, caught at different moments of the day and in different light. The artist had settled in Rome in 1895, where he had made friends with Duilio Cambellotti, Boccioni and Severini and revealed his adherence to the naturalistic and symbolist branch of Divisionism, in line with that of Segantini and Previati. In this phase, before he became an adherent of Futurism, of which he was one of the main exponents, the desire to produce «new» painting coincided with an orientation towards a faithful representation of reality, art interpreted in the dimension of the dynamic function of light, which led to a chromatic decomposition.

Renato Guttuso, The Crucifixion
Galleria Nazionale di Arte Moderna

«I've got to paint a picture on commission. It's been arranged by Cairola. The patron wants a crucifix to hang above the bed. How can he have a scene of torture suspended in his dreams? This is wartime: Abyssinia, gas, the gallows, decapitations, Spain, elsewhere. I want to paint this torment of Christ like a scene of today. Of course not in the sense of Christ dying every day on the cross for our sins... but as a symbol of all those who are subjected to insult, prison, torture for their ideas... the crosses (gallows) raised inside a room. The soldiers and the dogs – the dishevelled, scantily dressed, weeping women – in the candle light (the candle of Picasso's famous manifesto Guernica?), someone coming in and going out... or concentrate on contrast. Torture of the people with jugglers and soldiers. Circus and massacre.. ». The painting, finished in 1941, and exhibited for the Bergamo prize, was immediately attacked by the press of

the regime, who sensed its dramatically polemical vein. Considered one of the most important of Guttuso's masterpieces it is the painting which undoubtedly leaves its mark on the history of 20th century Italian art from the point of view of novelty of language. In fact, in the canvas, chromatic Expressionism exists side-by-side with plastic-geometric construction taken from Neo-Cubism.

Renzo Piano, Auditorium

For a long time, Rome suffered from the lack of an adequate venue for classical music events. This was remedied with the construction of the new Auditorium begun in 1994, which is considered today one of the most important venues in the world. The winning design in the international competition of 1994 bears the signature of Renzo Piano. The construction was finished in 2002. The site is in the gentle plane which extends from the banks of the Tiber and the Parioli Hill, between the Olympic Village, which was built for the 1960 games, the Palazzo dello Sport and the Stadio Flaminio planned by Pierluigi Nervi. Being outside the centre, the site has the advantage of being able to accommodate a large public influx with ease, and it also occupies a space which had long been a sort of artificial fracture, a hole in the city's structure. In the words of Renzo Piano, «The construction of a concert hall is the most wonderful adventure for an architect. It may be even more wonderful for a stringed instrument player to make a violin; but the activities are very similar, although the size and means may be different. In the end it's all about making instruments to make or to listen to music. The sound is the master; the sound box has to be able to vibrate with its frequencies and energy». The primary objective of his work is to define a new spatiality and it hinges on the ongoing relationship between man and nature, the space around him, the conditions it imposes and the materials, which are part of man's history and culture.

The Rome Auditorium is not merely an Auditorium, but a genuine City of Music. There are three distinct buildings, with different capacities, gathered around the focal point of a fourth open air theatre, a liveable urban space. On the roof of the complex there is a 38,000 square metre park, a further significant urban dimension to the adventure.

Richard Meier, Dives Misericordioso

Three white sails rising mysteriously, as if from an abandoned vessel stuck in the sand of a strange desert wall of anonymous palazzi, worn roads and uncultivated fields. Seen from a distance, this is the appearance of the church built by the American «star» Richard Meir, one of the most admired architects of the contemporary age, in the suburb of Tor Tre Teste. Far-away from every tourist itinerary, it was intended by the vicarship to be the Jubilee church. In 1996, the competition for the religious building, which was particularly wished for by Pope John Paul II, was announced. World-famous architects were invited to participate, including Tadao Ando, Gunther Behnisch, Santiago Calatrava, Peter Eisenman and Frank O. Gehry, all with the same objective: to build a parish church, which besides acting as a memorial for the Jubilee of 2000, would also be the visual equivalent of the contents of the Encyclical «Dives in Misericordia», issued by the pontiff in 1980. The winner of the competition, Richard Meier, put forward a plan which combines the functions of a place of welcome, gathering and religiosity, creating a structure which, in the bold forms and white materials, is intended to appear strongly evocative and symbolic. According to the architect himself, the sources of his inspiration were his Jewish, essentially aniconic religiosity, and the forms of the Italian Baroque. The architect summed up the project with the words, «This church is my masterpiece. It has been a unique venture; there was no model it could be based on». Stone is the material par excellence used by Meier. White and compact, it extends throughout the portico, floor and wall surfaces and even to the liturgical furnishings. The project was so original and demanding that it was a challenge even for Italian engineering. The only object taken faithfully from tradition is the large crucified Christ, a XVIIth century wooden work and a dominating, solemn presence in the church.

Via Appia Antica and Tomb of Cecilia

The ancient Roman road, which is extraordinarily well preserved and highly evocative, runs through the Parco Regionale dell'Appia Antica, a protected area established in 1988 for the preservation, discovery and enjoyment of this extraordinary heritage. Recent works have brought to light long tracts of the former road foundation of the Appia Antica, punctuated by memorial stones and monuments, symbols of great value in terms of history, landscape and culture. Among the various monuments which are strewn along the Appia Antica is the Tomb of Cecilia Metella. On the marble frieze, decorated with bucranes and festoons is the following inscription: Caecilia / Q. Cretici f. / Metella Crassi, identifying the deceased as Cecilia Metella, daughter of Quintus Metellus Cretious, consul in 69 BC and wife of Marcus Licinius Crassus, son of the famous Crassus, the contemporary of Caesar and Pompey. The majesty of the monument is in keeping with the importance of the woman to whom it was dedicated at the beginning of the Augustan age. The mausoleum consists of a square concrete base, originally faced in travertine, on top of which rests a circular drum, which is in turn covered with blocks of travertine. The attic storey, which is today decorated with a medieval crenellation, must originally have ended in a conical earth tumulus as in the mausoleum of Augustus, from which the architect of this tomb drew his inspiration.

Catacombs of Domitilla

The subsoil of the city of Rome is mainly tufaceous rock, which is very crumbly and easy to excavate, and full of underground tunnels which from antique times had been created for various purposes (hydraulic connections, tufa quarries, crypto-porticos of villas and burials). The Christians in Rome found these galleries the simplest solution for burials, which needed more space than the cremation traditionally used by the Romans up to the second century AD. According to an unfounded tradition, the catacombs, the Christian underground cemeteries, were supposed to have originated as a refuge from persecution. The immense network of catacomb galleries created space for thousands of tombs distributed in the walls and on the ground; the richest tomb was the arcosolium type, where the cavity was dug out of the tufa, closed with a slab and surmounted by an arch, which was usually decorated with frescoes. On the walls there were loculi, closed with tiles or marble and ornamented with permanently lit oil lamps. They only occasionally bore the name of the deceased. The catacombs were used as cemeteries up to the Vth century; they then became sanctuaries for martyrs, visited by pilgrims from all over Europe. From the IXth century, the relics of saints began to be moved from the primitive tombs to churches within the walls of the city. Gradually the entrances to the underground cemeteries disappeared and the catacombs were forgotten about and stayed undiscovered until the XVIth century, when Antonio Bosio initiated a systematic research. The catacomb of Domitilla, whose entrance is situated between Piazza dei Navigatori and the first part of Via Ardeatina, is one of the major underground cemeteries of Rome and was structured on top of pre-existing burial grounds. The land in this area belonged to Flavia Domitilla, niece of the consul, a noble Roman lady who was related to the Emperor Vespasian. Because of her Christianity, the Emperor banished her to exile in the Island of Ponza, where after a long martyrdom she eventually died.

Christ and the Apostles.
Catacombs of Domitilla.

The Good Shepherd.
Catacombs of Domitilla.

Index